The Tao
of Power

Also by Michael Page

The Power of Ch'i (Aquarian Press, 1988)

The Tao
of Power

MICHAEL PAGE

GREEN
PRINT

First published in 1989 by
Green Print
an imprint of The Merlin Press Ltd
10 Malden Road, London NW5 3HR

ISBN 1 85425 022 1

1 2 3 4 5 6 7 8 9 10 :: 99 98 97 96 95 94 93 92 91 90 89

Phototypeset by Input Typesetting Ltd, London in 10/12pt Sabon
Printed in England by Biddles Ltd., Guildford
on recycled paper

Contents

PART THREE: HOPE

Azure Dragon, White Tiger

*The image is clear: the greatest generation of ch'i [power]
occurs at the point where the loins of the dragon and the
tiger are locked together in intercourse.*
STEPHEN SKINNER

Throughout our lives our world changes: we are made aware
of annual cycles of fertile growth and fruitful death in which
there are rhythms of replenishment and renewal, decay and
death, of the sun rising and setting. Sometimes, in earthquake
and tempest, and in the miracle of conception and birth, we are
made aware of the awesome power of the Cosmos apparent in
these natural cycles of change.

I hope in this book to introduce an Eastern concept of the
laws that govern change and of the power behind them. In doing
so, I also hope to increase our understanding of how that power
may be controlled, and of how it has been harnessed by men
and women who have pursued the way of Taoism.

I shall examine our developed world today in the light of that
concept, whose main pillar has always been the maintenance of
harmony and balance.

Much of the book is about the growing problem of imbalance
in the material and spiritual world, and in the psyches of human
beings. Such imbalance grows steadily worse. It is apparent in
a decline in the quality of the environment, and a decline in the
quality of life in developed and developing nations. It is apparent
in the decline of religion as much as in the growth of consumerism. It is apparent in the failure of world leaders to respond
adequately to the needs of their followers.

Much change is taking place now: the world is becoming a
less predictable and more dangerous place.

Too often our view of change is that it is disordered and chaotic and that there is therefore a need to impose some order upon it. We ignore the probability that the chaos is a product of our ignorance of the need for careful balance. Because of our disregard for cosmic harmony we too often tackle the problems that arise by head-on attack, too often by means of dehumanized procedures and technological techniques alone, ignoring gentler pre-technological beliefs and practices that are different but at least as powerful.

What we in the developed countries, blocs and multinationals need to be aware of at all times is that the order we try to impose may not be consonant with fundamental cosmic laws, and that by ignoring them we may end up by causing disasters, sometimes on a world-wide scale.

A characteristic of change is that it is irreversible. Any return to pre-nuclear science is impossible, for instance. Once a change has occurred it is there to stay and affect all subsequent changes. It behoves us, therefore, to tread carefully.

As I shall try to show, it is in treading carefully and skilfully that Taoists excel.

The particular aspect of Taoism that I shall look at in these pages is the concept of positive and negative polarities known to the Chinese as *yin* and *yang*, as Azure Dragon and White Tiger, the tension between these two powerful polarities keeping the world in being. I shall describe various methods used for the management of this tension and the ways in which we may help or hinder that process.

More positively, then, it is a book about the need to maintain balance in all our endeavours. It is about the need for men and women to roll with the punches and to avoid head-on confrontation with nature and neuroses. In it I seek to take a fresh look at perennial problems from the viewpoint of this Taoist philosophy that has been studied, developed and followed by the Chinese for 3,000 years. Some of the practical aspects of this philosophy have lately begun to be revealed to the West in acupuncture and martial arts, and, in religion, has spread to the

West chiefly via Zen Buddhism. I hope to show that there may be other applications.

Following Part One, which looks at the basic concepts in more depth, I focus in Part Two on aspects of modern Western life in which balance is awry and suggest, none too confidently, paths towards increased harmony. In Part Three, which I've entitled 'Hope', I look at other areas of contemporary Western life in which some understanding of *yin/yang* balance already exists and in which there is some hope for increasing movement towards beneficial individual change and increased global understanding and harmony.

Finally, in my concluding chapter, I try to show how most men and many women in developed countries have been seduced by the one-sided power of positive thinking and action and consequently have ignored the more potent power that is revealed in the union of that positivity with its opposite.

Overall, I seek to describe ways in which an acquaintance with the love affair, sometimes peaceful, sometimes stormy, but always fruitful, of the Azure Dragon and his consort the White Tiger may help us to better order our lives both as individuals and as members of what may justly be described as a sick species on an ailing planet.

PART ONE

SAVING FACE

CHAPTER ONE

The Concept of Face

*The noble art of losing face
May one day save the human race.*
PIET HERN

The Chinese are adept at 'saving face', for they realize that the art of life is characterized by a delicate balancing act. The balance is between successfully weaving one's own individual way through life and the need for harmony and respect for others in the process.

As in market place haggling, so in personal relations, it is sometimes advantageous to step back so as to maintain the other's dignity in order to gain one's own ends.

The idea of saving face enshrines larger truths discovered long ago by Chinese Taoist Sages. That these truths are of value in modern life is my motive in writing this book. We live in an age whose philosophical and spiritual underpinnings are vastly different from those of ancient Chinese Taoist hermits or even from the stylized formality of the Confucian 'Superior Man'. The result is the mess in which we find ourselves.

In this chapter, I introduce fundamental Taoist beliefs that are illustrated by this peculiarly Chinese concept of 'face'.

Such a belief is that the immense power of the universe is kept in being by the interplay of positive and negative polarities, known as *yin* and *yang*.

The interplay of *yin* and *yang* involves a consideration of Change, which Taoists, and indeed the East generally, see as a cyclic rather than as a linear process. Change is inevitable. Whether the results of change for humanity are to be good or bad depends upon our attitudes to that change. Co-operation with the way of nature will lead to harmony with nature, while a disregard for the ways of nature, as we see all around us today, leads to disaster.

Control and co-operation with change is thus a prime concern of Taoism and this chapter includes a look at the *I Ching*, which may be seen as a technology that seeks to bring humanity into constructive relationship with the cosmic forces of change.

A WESTERN *YIN/YANG*

We begin with an example from a western study of child development as it is seen in the work of Jean Piaget, the great Swiss student of human cognitive development.

In Piaget's schema of the intellectual development of young children he speaks of living organisms' *adaptation* to the external in terms of a balance between *accommodation* and *assimilation*. Accommodation takes place in response to change. A tiger becomes hungry, seeks food, sees prey and kills. The killing is followed by assimilation: the food becomes part of the tiger, its hunger subsides, a balance is achieved and it has adapted to its circumstances. It is once more in a state of balance. Similarly, an intellectual quest will be accommodated to study, followed by assimilation of new knowledge, the whole process leading to new perceptions, and a recovery of balance as adaptation takes place.

In Taoist terms, the whole process is an example of the way in which the outgoing *yang* (hunger, the questing mind, the exploring body), is balanced by the inward-looking *yin* (digestion, absorption, appreciating the terrain), and how the resolution of their mutual tension results in a dynamic equilibrium.

One could perhaps compare the process to the irritation in the mollusc which results in a pearl. There is a bit of grit, and the innards of the creature accommodate to ease the irritation. The grit becomes assimilated into the inward workings of the mollusc and this results in adaptation, dynamic equilibrium, and an increase in beauty in the world.

In reading this book, you the reader will bring to it some

preconceptions of your own. These will be met, perhaps, with the new, and this meeting will cause some disequilibrium in your mind. You will accommodate your previous ideas to the new, seeking points of agreement and understanding. If that can be achieved, there follows an assimilation of the new into the old, forming a new equilibrium: you will feel more at ease, and perhaps look forward to the next disequilibrium.

Writing the book involves a similar process. I sit down to write this chapter, with certain pre-set ideas from previous writing on the subject. I turn to a reference book to confirm a point, or to find an apt quotation. My eye is caught by some new idea, or a sentence which amplifies or (horror!) contradicts my theme. I pause and accommodate myself to the new, assimilate it, and experience that happy feeling of creative equilibrium.

Having written those words, I find myself pausing. 'Creative equilibrium': from where did that phrase spring? I search my mind. I feel somewhat destabilized, and realise that I could (should?) now spend some time in delving into the whole process of creativity. I decide to let it go, but find myself sitting again with my hands on my head, gazing emptily at the wall opposite.

I know that as I go on writing or make another cup of coffee the disequilibrium will persist until something I write or read or otherwise experience will somehow and perhaps synchronistically lead to a new equilibrium.

(This illustrates a Taoist faith that the cosmos – the *Tao* – is ready to aid the process of enlightenment, and illustrates the consequent belief that letting things flow unconcernedly but with alert mindfulness will bring about balance, much as water finds its own level, or as an infant playfully explores its environment. This idea – which the Chinese call *wu wei* – will be met with again later in this chapter and frequently throughout this book.)

A young child spends all its time achieving a growing balance between desire and the hard reality of the world around. The child learns to accept the environment and learns to organize behaviour in order to make allowances for occasional environmental intractability. All normal growing children come to realize that they cannot pass through a closed door: they accommodate to this feature of the environment. Later, by assimilation, they learn to open the door: to change the environment to suit their behaviour. The two processes are never independent: child and environment are in a continuous state of interaction which maintains the state of adaptation.

It was Pavlov who first called the process one of maintaining *dynamic equilibrium*. This phrase calls to mind the careful balancing act of a tightrope walker, adapting every move, and every move of the wire, to survival. We human beings have been likened to survival machines and as such we survive through maintaining balance. Adults, like children, live in a continuous state of seeking to maintain a condition of dynamic equilibrium. Sometimes, like children, we are skilful, sometimes not. A young child who persisted in trying to butt its head through the closed door would be acting unskilfully: indeed, an observer would be justified in regarding the child with some anxiety as to its intellectual capacity even at an early age. Is there so much difference between the child butting the door with its head and humankind stock-piling nuclear weapons, or creating deadly radioactive waste with a half-life longer than our entire previous tenure of the planet?

In the arms race, a state of dynamic equilibrium is constantly being attained, seldom by much process of ratiocination, and will be maintained for as long as the environment (which includes the other superpowers and powers on the planet) does not become so intractable that no other recourse than head butting will be felt to be desirable. But clearly this balance, this equilibrium, is indeed dynamic, is liable to change, and if the only *yin/yang* balance that is possible is the insensibility of the human race, then what is that to the eternal *Tao*?

This Chinese word *Tao* is one we shall meet repeatedly. It is sometimes translated 'way', but in fact it is not satisfactorily fully translatable. As the *Tao Te Ching* says, 'The *Tao* that can be named is not the eternal *Tao*' – a full definition misses the point . . . Sufficient for our purposes now is to say that it is a concept that may be seen to approximate to the plenum, that is, to space completely filled with matter, or to 'the ground of all being', expressing itself to our senses in terms of energy, which the Chinese called *ch'i*.

There is no situation involving animate or inanimate phenomena in which a continual process of adaptation is not going on. From the formation, erosion and recreation of mountain ranges, the birth, flowing and extinction of galaxies to the petty daily affairs of people there is no situation in which a balance within change is not being sought. There is thus no situation in which people are found where they do not desire an easing of the tension between their will to live and enjoy, and the intractability of the environment (which includes other people's wills to live and enjoy).

EASTERN *YIN/YANG*

The maintenance of dynamic balance is fundamental to Taoist belief and practice.

Two thousand years before Christ, the Yellow Emperor, a founding father of Taoism, is said to have pronounced on what he saw as the primary law of life: that all beings and things were in a permanent state of cyclic change, dynamic tension and ongoing transformation. *Ch'i*, the basic energy of the *Tao*, continually streamed forth. From it all things emerged, and into it all things ultimately returned.

In an ancient Chinese text it is written, '*Yin/yang* is the way of heaven and earth, the fundamental principle of the myriad things, the father and mother of change and transformation, the root of inception and destruction.' The myriad things, sometimes called the 'ten thousand things', are the whole of differentiated phenomena; the material universe is kept in existence in dynamic equilibrium by the twin forces of *yin* and *yang*. The continuous creation of the ten thousands thing is the function of these two forces. (See Figure One).

Similarly, Chapter 42 of the *Tao Te Ching* says: 'All things

Figure 1. *The Yin-Yang diagram, symbol of the two great balancing forces that keep the universe in being. The dynamic tension between them is apparent in the seed of change contained in each.*

are backed by shade (*yin*) and faced by light (*yang*) and harmonized by the immaterial breath' (*ch'i*).

The interplay of these two, *yin* and *yang*, is accepted as pervading the everyday life of Chinese men and women of all walks of life.

In Chinese Taoist art, for example, the heavy is always in tension with the light, and the resolution of the two is a lively balance in the eye of the beholder, springing from the mind and skill of the artist.

In the Chinese art of *T'ai Chi Ch'uan*, for another example, or indeed in any other form of martial art, there is a constant tension between positive and negative, between going forwards and going back.

12

In every aspect of life, formal and informal, the interplay of *yin* and *yang* may be taken account of. Such interplay may be gentle or it may be violent: the explosive energy sometimes released in the vicinity of a martial arts master is truly impressive.

'Harmony' as a word has gentle overtones, but it is worth emphasizing at this point that the process of achieving harmony is not necessarily gentle. It is true that Taoists see themselves as gentle beings who tend to retire from the world. They are, nevertheless, not surprised that dynamic equilibrium may sometimes be achieved through sudden, violent and cataclysmic change. Nor are they averse to this: they merely try to ensure that their actions are always appropriate to the changes they see evolving.

CYCLES OF CHANGE

They are helped in this because the law of *yin* and *yang* is paralleled by another law: this law being that change is cyclic.

A human existence is cyclic, not linear as in the seven ages of Shakespeare's man. This is seen in the Buddhist conception of conditioned co-production, and, indeed in the whole generalized Eastern belief in *karma* and rebirth. All manifestations, from wave-particle to human to galaxy, endure a regular cycle of birth, growth, decay and death, followed by rebirth, growth, decay, death *ad infinitum*. This is by no means to say that the succeeding cycles are identical: the essence of rebirth is that change is implied. Even though Taoists tend not to believe in a succession of lives, but in immortality in this one, they do believe in the possibility of perfection through controlling change in the successive moment-by-moment rebirths that make up this one life.

The concept of cyclic repetition is worth bearing in mind when considering the process of maintaining dynamic equilibrium. As with the mills of God, the grinding is thorough and certain and may be very slow. The balance may be long in coming, but come it surely will.

That having been said, a practical consequence follows. Whether aiming for future advantageous rebirth or present-life immortality it seems wise for an individual to instigate very little: whatever is commenced should be continued with utmost caution.

One should practice *wu wei* (non-action), which means one should avoid planning and striving, but move watchfully with the flow of circumstances as they arise.

It is because of this latter belief in the virtue of *wu wei* that there arose the mistaken idea that Taoism is excessively passive, concerned only with observing the flowers and growing the herbs, and withdrawing from the life and concerns of fellow people. But nature can be violent, with earthquakes and typhoons redressing stresses and strains. Similarly, a Sage, an enlightened being, can act violently when following the flow of arising circumstances. A Sage's activity in detecting, aiding, and abetting the flow of change, will, however, be as selfless as that of an earthquake: if fellow human beings choose to misinterpret either, they are free to be in error. The Sage will not have set the process in action, but will have joined with it as an active participant rather than as a passive observer.

Everything, then, is subject to cyclic change controlled by *yin* and *yang*. Any interference in the harmonious resolution of tension between the two will be destructive of beings, objects, systems and empires, either in the short or the long term. Not only do men and women need to subject themselves to the law, but they need, as conscious beings, to search for, to exemplify, and to augment the possibility of harmony between opposites, because all opposites partake of the universal nature of *yin* and *yang*. That this view has implications for social coexistence, the overcoming of prejudice, the increase of tolerance, wise government and so forth hardly needs emphasizing.

The life-style of the Taoist Sage arises from and reinforces practical wisdom in all areas of social life as well as in personal development.

There are many practices by which the Taoist seeks to attain wisdom. All of them have been practised for centuries: their strangeness to sophisticated westerners in no way invalidates the undoubted success that attends them.

THE *I CHING*

One of the most important ways to wisdom and everyday practicality is in detecting and going with the flow of circumstances. In this it is necessary to know in what way circumstances are flowing in relation to oneself.

A technique by which the Chinese sought – and still seek – to slot into the process of cyclic change in the universe, to align him or herself with the flow of events, and to become, as it were, one with the heavens, was to use methods of divination.

The best-known in the West is the *I Ching*. This ancient oracle, 'The Book of Changes', is exactly what its name implies. It illustrates the process of cyclic change, and does this by means of hexagrams that are made up of combinations of representations of *yin* and *yang*. (See Figure Two).

The method of divination can be illustrated by means of an example from modern life, and to this end I thought it permissible to consult the *I Ching* in just such a way as did Carl Jung and John Blofeld when they first met the oracle.

I asked a question such as might concern a modern business man. It was, 'Should I buy these shares?'

Briefly the hexagrams were arrived at as follows. Three coins were let fall: if there were two or three heads uppermost, a *yang* (unbroken) line was written down. Two or three tails indicated *yin*, and a broken line was written. Six such lines were arrived at, and were written from the bottom up.

Using this method, Hexagram A was arrived at.

In this, the fifth line from the bottom was arrived at by having three heads fall: such a strong *yang* line will inevitably soon turn to *yin*, and is of great significance in the interpretation of the hexagram.

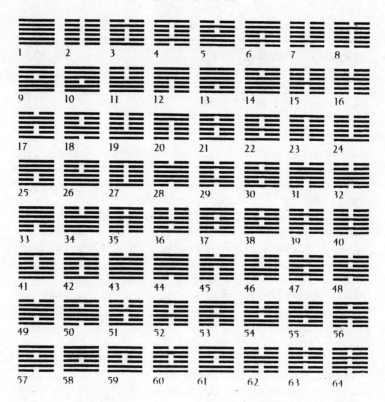

Figure 2. *The hexagrams in the order in which they appear in the* I
Ching. Yang *lines are unbroken,* yin *lines are broken.*

Hexagram A

Hexagram B

Using John Blofeld's translation,[1] the basic hexagram is Number 31, entitled 'Attraction, Sensation'. The text reads: 'Attraction: Success! Righteous persistence brings reward. Taking a wife will result in good fortune.' It appears from this that there is a very positive indication that the shares should be bought. The reference to take a wife has a number of meanings: it could here refer to the embracing of opposites, achieving balance, and not going too bull-headed at things. The omens are, on the whole, favourable thus far.

However, there is that 'moving' second line, and the commentary on that is: 'Sensation in the legs – misfortune! good fortune comes to those who do not venture forth.' To avoid the implications of the word 'misfortune' would be most unwise. Caution is indicated, then.

Taking it all in all, perhaps this whole divination may mean that it is a good time to buy, but that inevitable change will be for the worse – a presaging of a market crash, perhaps.

There is a Commentary in the *I Ching* on the basic text of this hexagram, and one of the things that is said is, 'The inner nature of everything in heaven and earth can be gauged by observing what it is that stimulates each of them.' A suggestion perhaps that further investigation of the opposites, the pros and cons, would be worth while. Caution again.

Finally a note on the symbolism of the hexagram says, 'In dealing with men, the Superior Man shows himself to be entirely void of selfishness.' This appears to indicate that selfless behaviour, such as spreading the word, would be advantageous.

When the line has moved, the *I Ching* indicates the possible future consequences. The new hexagram is number 62. (See Hexagram B).

This hexagram is entitled 'The Small Get By', and its text is this: 'The small get by – success! Persistence in a righteous course brings reward. Small things can be accomplished now, but not great ones. When birds fly high, their singing is out of tune. The humble, but not the mighty, are favoured now with great good fortune.'

So the canny investor has a wealth of information: nothing

definite, but enough to enable a wise decision to be made in line with changing circumstances. It is all eminently sensible and pragmatic, which is certainly what the Chinese would expect of the *I Ching*.

CONCLUSION

Change is inevitable. Like a surf-rider, the Sage goes with change to best advantage, secure in the knowledge that by conforming to the will of heaven, there will be benefit to all: Sage, fellow human beings and the cosmos as a whole.

The essence of practising Taoism is to try by every means at one's disposal to arrive at universal harmony – and this is an internal process. As we shall see in succeeding chapters, such harmony is to be aimed at in one's personal life style, in one's physical well-being, in relation to one's neighbour, in relation to one's environment, and in relation to the cosmos. Its practice involves mindfulness, fitness of body and openness of spirit.

Taoism is a pragmatic philosophy, as befits the Chinese. It does not spout forth high-minded sentiments without demonstrating the very real practical advantages to be gained from observing its precepts. What can possibly go awry for the man or woman who conforms to the natural flow of events in their life? Those events are both material and psychological. The really healthy and whole human is a unity: mental, physical, spiritual and cosmological aspects working as one, each reinforcing the other.

To help people to observe the Taoist precepts, practical aids are provided. We have seen one of them, the *I Ching*, and we shall see others: alchemical practices, sexual techniques, observation of the *yin* and *yang* in the landscape, all of them put to daily use by Taoists in their urgent desire to achieve their life's ambitions. Such ambitions range from moving towards the wisdom of the Sage to picking a congenial spouse, from attaining longevity to making a killing at the races, and certainly includes advice on 'face'.

The subtle art of face-saving is based on a fundamental Taoist belief that the entire cosmos is held together by the tension between positive and negative forces, between *yin* and *yang*, those Chinese words under which all opposites are subsumed. Without the constant interplay between *yin* and *yang*, between all opposite polarities, the social fabric is rent, to say nothing of individuals and universe.

A search for universal harmony and equilibrium has consequently been a constant preoccupation of Taoists. Only through attaining harmony within individuals and in their relationships may humankind, they think, aid the general process of cosmic change. The two are identical: by living in balanced and respectful harmony with our neighbour and our neuroses we aid the universal process.

It is therefore not only bad form to cause another to lose face, it is unwise. To cause another's loss of face implies that one has gone too far, has lost balance, and is likely to fall on one's own face. This is likely to be quite literally true in that typically Eastern activity of martial art.

No one can say that we are living balanced lives in a balanced world: in every field of human endeavour, we seem to have lost that sense of respect for ourselves and our surroundings which marked (and still marks) more primitive people. Taoists believe even inanimate objects share with us the living power of the cosmos which they called *Tao*, and which manifests itself in *yin/yang* balance. We go too far, losing our collective and individual balance in a most unseemly way in most of our endeavours, and look as never before as though we shall at any moment fall on our collective face in a polluted and radioactive mud of our own making.

Every human activity without exception requires for its achievement a balancing of positive with negative forces. Even such a mundane matter as walking illustrates the principle. To walk is a matter of alternate imbalance and balance: a forging forward, followed by consolidation, the whole being a balanced process of dynamic equilibrium.

We have largely forgotten that we are creatures whose

survival as a species has depended on such a balance between development and status quo. We share this characteristic with all other living species and with the whole of creation.

Yet our collective amnesia is not complete: the cosmic truth that our very existence depends upon the maintenance of a dynamic balance between opposites continues to poke its head upward as if inviting our earnest attention, as we shall see repeatedly throughout this book.

Each individual is part of the total cosmos, partaking in the ebb and flow of its energies as seen in the cyclic procession of events in the interplay of the *yin* and the *yang*. Taoists (and often non-Taoists) believe most fervently, from careful observation of the way things are going at any particular moment of time, that all such ambitions from the most mundane to the most elevated are indeed attainable in this life.

In Part Two of the book, I look at four areas of human experiences in which imbalance is apparent. The first of these is one which, in the West, has been out of kilter for centuries.

PART TWO

DISCORD

Harmony would lose its attractiveness if it did not have a background of discord.
TEHYI HSIEH

CHAPTER TWO

Azure Dragon Rampant

Let us imagine it is January of next year.

Christmas is over yet again. Wrapped in tissue paper, the Christ Child is lain to rest with the plastic cattle, cardboard angels, Joseph and Mary.

All nice and straightforward, this has been, a pleasantly traditional story of a remarkable conception, followed by a humble birth: both preceding a remarkable life. But why confuse the children with the virgin birth? What is all this about Mary?

She is, of course, the *yin* White Tiger, the seed pearl of balancing change.

The present chapter is about this principle of dynamic balance lying at the heart of Taoist practice, a principle which is present but largely unrecognized within most organized religions.

To a true Taoist, organized religion is anathema. Yet it is true that dotting the Chinese countryside were numerous Taoist temples, practising the worship of a pantheon of gods, presided over by a hierarchical priesthood. Such perversions of an original simplicity are not unique to Taoism. What is almost unique is that its fundamental simplicity remained, hidden away in the vast countryside of China, where it is hoped there may still exist hermitages in which the old Taoism is practised. And if that is a false hope, then there are always the hearts of the Chinese people, steeped in race-memories and reminded in everyday life of the universality of the principle that the cosmos is kept in being by a dynamic balance of opposing tensions.

This fundamental bipolarity is depicted in Taoism in a variety of ways, not least in the union of the sexes: the union of the male Azure Dragon and the female White Tiger. Their union illustrates the balance between *yin* and *yang* forces that keeps creation in being.

It is apparent to any observer that the loss of such a balance seen in the rape of the forests, the stockpiling of armaments and such like, is in danger of tipping the inhabitants of this planet over the brink of disaster. The developed and developing nations disregard the White Tiger's place in the scheme of things: to their peril, for tigers, too, have claws.

THE WHITE TIGER IN CHRISTIANITY

We in the West, heirs of the Christian tradition, are up to our necks in a mire which is entirely of our own making, stemming as it does from our seeming inability to control our appetites for more food, more goods, more of our kind, more of everything. We are not ruthless enough with ourselves when it comes to satisfying our next whim for a chocolate eclair, another nuclear warhead. Such whims are childish, and like childish whims are apparently to be satisfied immediately, with no doubt that they can be satisfied – at a cost.

What cost? Oh, just the future of the planet, our children, a million Ethiopians. Pass the plate.

All of this can be described in terms of an overbalance in the direction of *yang* activity. This thought has been summed up by Robert Graves, who suggests that we are now, for all practical purposes, ruled by the *yang* sun-god Apollo, armed with a thermonuclear bomb as his thunderbolt.

Yet in the *I Ching* we see how an over-powerful *yang* presaged a return to *yin*.

Mary has always been there, the object of devotion to millions of Roman Catholics, mediating on their behalf with her Son and the Father. In Taoist terms we would say that she has provided a *yin* counterbalance in an otherwise male-dominated religion.

Lack of balance in a family can lead to stress: a father bringing up children without a mother-figure finds it difficult. Can it be that the Christian church has come to realize this in its own housekeeping? Perhaps it is ready to re-cognize the value of a necessary tension between opposites that keeps creation creating and families in being.

There are faint signs of a sea-change in the Christian world. The ordination of women in the Church of England may be a result of the feminist movement. It may be something else. And what is the Pope doing, collecting Marian shrines worldwide? Why has he added an 'M' to his coat of arms?

Perhaps the Christian Church is about to return to earlier ways, responding to the unconscious pressure of cosmic *yin/yang* forces, and recognizing again the influence of pre- and extra-Christian truths about the need to have the stern father's rule balanced by Woman, the mother, the consort, the alter ego.

But in Christianity and in Islam, the male principle, *yang*, has typically dominated. Why?

Perhaps it was from the harshness of life in the desert, under the burning heat of the sun, that the masculine religions grew, pushful, aggressive and conquering. To thrust and to be active, is to make a mark, and be more easily placed in a hostile world. To be retiring, nurturing, and receptively supportive in such an environment is to have difficulty in being recognized as of worth, and hence to have difficulty in seeing oneself as of worth.

Whatever the reason, there is no doubt that the patriarchal Father has usurped the position of the matriarchal Mother, and pushed her into and beyond the sidelines. The masculine solar consciousness, left-hemisphered, abstract and conceptual, became overdeveloped in the desert lands and in the lands their people conquered and colonized, at the expense of the feminine consciousness. Like their women, the White Tiger was put in actual or psychological purdah, and throughout the centuries, even in territory far removed from the desert, their women have been pushed to the background, removed from the councils of men.

But the White Tiger is there all the same, and has claws, a fact of which the Azure Dragon is always mindful in the dark recesses of his subconscious.

25

A PSYCHOANALYTIC VIEW

Men and women, particularly in the west, turn their backs to the White Tiger, and suffer a typical neurosis as a result.

Men and women at an early stage of their life go in fear of mother – much as they must as a species have feared the Earth-mother in primitive times. She (or her breast) is early realized to be the centre and fulcrum of an easily snuffed-out life. If Melanie Klein and other neo-Freudians are to be believed, each of us has to go through a stage of fearing and wishing to destroy our mother, a wish so terrible that it is relegated to the unconscious. It is a stage at which many are fixated for life.

According to this view, it is no wonder that we accept the view of the feminine as being negative and evil, no wonder that the monster that holds the Tibetan Wheel of Life is female, no wonder that we prefer to see ourselves as the children of a father-god. Religions reflect this syndrome, and even non-theistic traditional Buddhism is by no means guiltless. The Buddha is reputed to have said, 'It is impossible, it cannot happen that a women Arahant should be a complete and perfect Buddha . . . it cannot be.' Yet, as we shall see, in Buddhism, as in Christianity, the reverse of the coin is present. Mahayana Buddhism, too, has an aspect of the Enlightened Ones that is female, and who has sworn to be eternally female.

Most men and women, particularly in the West, go through their lives never developing beyond a stage of infantile behaviour in which they turn away from the god-mother: the god-father at least appears to offer the hope of forgiveness: it seems that the mighty breast that can be taken away for ever is not so forgiving. Western men and women, if they worship at all, do not seek to worship the Earth-mother, or her qualities, because if the insights of psychoanalysis have any validity, they have to go through a stage in this life (or another) of cutting loose from her before final enlightenment. In that enlightenment they see the truth of their membership one of another, and consequently, their need for the female aspect of humanity within.

Few people reach such a stage. Most remain at the infantile

stage, and are encouraged to regard the female as specifically evil and dangerous, as witness the witch burnings of our recent history. It is noteworthy that in the East such fearsome aspects of the feminine principle as, for example, Kali have not been put beyond the pale, but have been drawn into the orthodox pantheons. No such resolution is apparent in the West, to its loss.

In the West, all power rests with the preferred father, and religion, where it is practised, remains *yin*-denying and patriarchal. Yet God did not create himself in a man's image; people did that. And now they have gone further: they have attempted to usurp His powers. In such hubris, they no longer appear to have any fear of the elemental forces of the earth. Have they not created primitive life, split the atom? Do they not have the earth at their mercy? The emphasis on patriarchy has had results that are ripening at an exponential rate in our own day. The tendency has been growing for centuries until today Prometheus is truly unbound.

Yet *yin* is here, in the West, waiting, underground, perhaps just now emerging from a couple of millennia of undervaluation, just in time, hopefully, to save the coming harvest.

The wisdom is there, beneath the surface within us and in our culture.

A HISTORICAL VIEW

In Britain, the religion of long standing was that often subsumed in common memory under the name of the Druids. Many of the characteristics of this religion are lost in the mists of time, hidden still further by the fog of romantic nonsense written in the last couple of hundred years. Nevertheless, the Druids seem to have had a reverential and balanced attitude to nature, their fellow life-forms, and the feminine principle.

Some of the earliest archaeological artefacts and earliest mythologies indicate that a very primitive concept of the deity was in fact female, that there lay in certain early religious impulses

27

the idea of the earth as a mighty womb. Even today, as in pre-history, the idea of the earth being fertilized by the semen of the gods in the form of rain is said to underlie much primitive religious belief.

Men and women as hunter-gatherers followed a balanced line: aware that they were maintained in existence by acting in concert with the earth and its other inhabitants. With the beginning of primitive agriculture, a change came about: they became more aware of their *yang* power to act on the world, operating on the earth rather than co-operating with the earth and elements. They were uneasily aware, through storm, tempest and other upheavals, that any control was at its best tenuous: all fruits sprang from the womb of earth. They were in the final analysis at the mercy of elementals.

So our own ancestors felt that adherence to the will of nature and the gods, as far as it could be discerned, should be the prudent rule to follow.

When Christianity came to the British Isles, the Celtic Christians adapted characteristics of the old ways to the contours of the new. They continued to believe that the will of God should emerge in their reverence for nature and the rhythms and harmonies of the natural environment. If these were carelessly or deliberately flouted they continued to believe that disaster was bound to result; whereas great good was sure to come of their observance. In all of this, the harshness of the desert was nowhere apparent.

They seem to have been spiritual precursors of the gentle St Francis in their love of animals: in none of the early stories of Celtic Saints do we hear of them being anything other than gentle: there was none of the arrogance towards the animal creation that reaches its nadir in battery farming in our own age. They had an affinity to these, their fellow creatures: they might rebuke them, but they were never cruel or even discourteous to them. This delightful affinity between human and animal was much closer than the master/slave relationship that developed civilizations have adopted. They do not appear to have regarded animals as some kind of self-animated clockwork.

(A process we seek to reverse now when we present our children with teddy bears with tape recorders hidden in the tummies that used only to contain, at most, a squeaker.)

Most importantly from our point of view, they appear to have been fully aware of the need to preserve the feminine aspect of God.

Throughout early history, the Earth Mother had been accorded more reverence than any male deity – a *yin* imbalance that was to be corrected with the passage of time. But before the rise of *yang*, there had been in Mesopotamia, for instance, a belief in a suffering god dying annually and passing into the land of darkness from which he was rescued by his spouse/mother-goddess. In Crete was found Minoa, and a Mother-goddess cult. And in Celtic Christian Britain, persisting in folk-wisdom as providing a necessary balance, was found the Holy Brigid.

In her life she was an abbess. On her death she seems soon to have been taken up and developed in much the same way as happened to Gautama the Buddha, and to the Mahayana Buddhist deity, the Lady Tara. Like these two, she was revered as a trinity.

Firstly, she was recognized as having been human, and thus was able to share people's tribulations. Secondly she was seen as the primeval earth-mother – Robert Graves considered her to be the mother of all the gods – and, thirdly, as the heavenly provider. In the latter role she was seen as offering herself as a guide to men and women by which they could reach towards enlightenment.

The wisdom is there, in our national religious history. It is there, too, in the wider historical and contemporary religious world.

THE WHITE TIGER IN BUDDHISM

Similar to Brigid, Celtic representative of the Earth-Mother, and worked out in far more detail by the advanced thinkers of Mahayana Buddhism, there is the Lady Tara. This Tibetan

Vajrayana deity has three aspects to her, each one suitable for the needs of her worshippers.

Firstly, she must once have been a being like ourselves, who, through long ages of practising the path of the Bodhisattva, attained to perfect enlightenment. When she took the Bodhisattva Vow to work unceasingly for the final enlightenment of all beings and to renounce entry to Nirvana until that day arrived, she departed from the usual form. Instead of vowing to return in future births in a male form, she took the opposite as her vow. She would work for others only in the form of a woman.

In this manifestation, that of Bodhisattva, she is called Mother of all the Buddhas, and The Saviouress. As such, she has always been associated with being able to help those who worship her in affairs of the world.

Secondly, she is identified as the Mother Goddess, and represents the Universal Mother to be found supporting all religions. In this identification, she has three aspects. One of these is as Goddess of the Underworld, ruling the demons of the hells, in modern parlance those demons of the psyche such as greed and avarice. In this aspect she also has control of rebirths. Another of her aspects is as the Goddess of the Earth, ruling all plants, animals and human beings. Her domination of wild animals symbolizes the possibility of her restraining the instinctual drives in the human psyche. She also represents the Goddess of the Heavens, the Sophia, the Goddess of Wisdom, the source of vision and symbol, of law, of ritual, of poetry, and all those things that give direction to the life of human beings.

Thirdly, she is a Complete and Perfect Buddha, and Goddess of Action. In the latter aspect she is able to act with lightning swiftness to help those who call on her in dire distress.[1]

It is strange that Tibet should have been saving up this markedly feminine form of Enlightened Being, ready for the time that has now come when Tibetan Buddhism is spreading throughout an increasingly feminist world in the age, long foretold by them, when iron birds would fly.

She appears to be a deity tailor-made for providing a *yin* input to this *yang*-suffering world. But we shall do well to remember that she has a dual role, well exemplified in the Hindu Goddess, Kali the Destroyer, possessor of characteristics such as are found in Nature herself, which can be as ruthlessly destructive as it is unstintingly benevolent. The Tiger has claws.

Kwan-yin is another manifestation of the Earth-mother, here from the Chinese Buddhist tradition. She too has the two aspects of creator and destroyer, life-giver and death-dealer, holding within herself the tension of opposites which is the process of transformation through Wisdom and Method (*yin* and *yang*) into the ultimate unity, Nirvana, or the *Tao*. Like Brigid and Tara, she is both Queen of Heaven and the Great Earth Mother, The Tellus Mater, from whom, echoing the *Tao*, all things are born and to whom all return. If she can be cruel and ruthless and fearful she is yet 'kind and gentle and indulgent, ever a handmaid in the service of mortals . . .'

THE WHITE TIGER MATES

Taoism is a practical and pragmatic belief system, eschewing theory in favour of practice whenever possible.

One of the ways in which Taoists believe that individual and cosmic balance can be attained is through ritual (and ordinary) union of male and female. They believe that the harmony of the *Tao* and the controlling of its urgent creative power is achieved through sexual union. Sexual union, in fact, has been a feature of Taoist strivings towards the perfection of the Immortals, and is similarly the route towards the achievement of enlightenment in Tantrik Hinduism and Buddhism. Tantrism, indeed, sets women on high, sometimes higher than men. 'Buddhahood abides in the female organ' it is said in a triumphant advancement of the *yin* principle. This contrasts with the unsurprising practice of celibacy found in *yang*-dominated religions.

The sex act, as well as being, quite rarely, a spiritual ritual, is also, most commonly, of the earth, earthy. It figures largely in the everyday life of us ordinary people: much of our emotional life is occupied with satisfying the need we feel for another of the opposite sex, or, if we are gay, for a partner who can similarly complement our own strengths with weakness, and our weaknesses with strength. It is a longing for completeness that motivates the urge, an urge which is in a very real sense primeval.

This urge presses a return to psychic balance.

We need, as a Western people, to foster this same urge towards balance in union with the great, dark, warm, indwelling Earth-Mother that our ancestors knew and worshipped.

The Universal Mother is an archetype, and so is to be found lurking in humankind's collective unconsciousness and in all religions. In Europe, besides Mary and Brigid, she has been known as Mother of the Gods, Minerva, Venus, Diana, Proserpine, Ceres, Juno, Hecate, and Isis. Her typical form is that of a beautiful and slender woman, pale with long golden hair and blue eyes, though she is also seen in the form of a hag, or as an animal such as an owl, mare, sow or raven.

In Asia, her names include Tara, Kuan-yin, Kali, Vaishno Devi and Durga. Again, she is not always benign. She can take many forms and many colourings, and both human and part-human shape.

The earth appeared to our very early ancestors to give of her bounty in the same mysterious way as women gave birth. Little wonder, then, that matriarchies were common: the female principle seemed paramount. Even when farming emerged and the connection between the sexual act and reproduction became clear, and when men's part in the generative process was recognized, their share was still seen as insignificant compared to that of women.

Taoists recognized, long before Freud, that men as a sex have always secretly been frightened of their *yin* partners, women, and have consequently feared the cosmic creative power hinted at in the act of reproduction. Even though this fear is largely underground at the present time, and *yang* appears paramount, yet at some level (generally unconscious) we realize fearfully that the balance will be restored, that the Goddess must assume her rightful place, and we fear that the longer this takes, the less merciful will be her face when it is revealed to us.

It is this submerged knowledge that keeps the majority of ordinary individuals in the 'developed' countries carefully worried and which restrains them from whole-hearted acceptance of the seeming cornucopia of goodies that daily pours upon them. Deep down, there is the knowledge that if a balance is to be restored, one of the aspects of the Earth Mother, Queen of Heaven, is that of Kali, Hindu goddess of death and destruction. It is this unconscious knowledge that is another of the root causes of the endemic existential *angst* that afflicts us all.

Such cosmic forces will out: they will not be gainsaid for ever. Until recently, this has been acknowledged by humanity at large. It still is recognized in many so called primitive parts of the world, until the bulldozers flatten the knowledge along with the trees.

CONCLUSION

Truly, many and varied are the ways in which men and women strive religiously towards the goal of peace and enlightenment. This chapter has tried to show that such goals are attainable only through the balance of *yin* and *yang*, and the reintroduction to *yang*-dominated religion of the Earth Goddess, Earth-mother, Mary, Tara, Brigid, or whatever she may be called.

People can, given the will, choose to co-operate with *yin* forces and return to the state in which, once upon a time, they were able, psychologically and politically, openly to worship the Great Earth Mother, dark, damp, and nurturing. Perhaps, at some deep level of their psyche, people are doing so: such an effort, even if unconscious, will have effects at the conscious level. Superficially, this may emerge as a return to healthy eating and living, ecological awareness, a growing respect for the folk wisdom of developing countries, and the like. Certainly there is a tide flowing: the Earth-Mother will support the weary swimmer.

We let John Allegro have the penultimate word:

> It may be that despite our rightly prized rationality, religion still offers Man his best chance of survival . . . It must be a faith that offers something more than a formal assent to a set of highly speculative dogma . . . It must promise its adherents a living relationship that answers Man's individual needs within a formal structure of communal worship. It has to satisfy the emotions without violating the believer's intellectual integrity . . . Historically, the cult of the Earth-Mother has probably come nearest to fulfilling this role, and, being sexually oriented, it has been specially concerned with this . . . element in Man's biological constitution. Perhaps in our present concern for ecological conservation . . . we are moving towards a revival of the old Nature religion . . . [2]

Alternatively, we may be moving towards adopting many of the beliefs and practices of Taoism, in which sexuality, a living relationship with nature, conservation, intellectual integrity and rationality, indeed, all of the 'ten thousand things' may be harmoniously balanced, to the advantage of all.

Among those practices is one aimed at enlightenment, at individual autonomy. Our age, as I describe in the next chapter, is characterized by increasing difficulty for the average man or woman in finding their own authentic identity.

CHAPTER THREE

The Sage

Too many people live lives 'of quiet desperation'. This need not be, and should not be. Each of us has the right and the ability to lead a life of balanced happiness.

Most men and women today are never happy for long. This is because they see their identity as being bound up in the outer world of impermanent things – the 'world of the ten thousand things' as Taoists describe the phenomenal world. The consumer society feeds this unhappy tendency by providing ever more objects to be acquired, and by contriving to set up a gnawing feelings of unease and anxiety until they are acquired. All this has been documented again and again, and its results – alienation, consumerism, the society of the spectacle and so on – have all been described. There is a giddy chasing of the tail.

This chapter will rely to a great extent on Lao Tsu's book, the *Tao Te Ching*. This ancient Chinese classic is the distillation of Lao Tsu's wisdom in 5000 characters. Little is known of Lao Tsu, a retiring man, except for the fact that he produced this little gem of enigmatic wisdom and is generally regarded as the founding father of Taoist philosophy. Roughly translated as 'The Book of the Way', the *Tao Te Ching* sets out to help its reader to tread the way of life happily and therefore considerately. It is a handbook for those aspiring to become more happy, self-realized, autonomous beings – Sages.

Chapter 44 of the *Tao Te Ching* says: 'Over-love of anything will lead to wasteful spending; amassed riches will be followed by heavy plundering.' Over-love of things is no modern phenomenon, but what appears to be an innate tendency of humanity that has gone to an extreme in our age.

It is not innate, however. Humankind is capable of improvement. Individuals are able even in this day and age to approach a state akin to the happy Taoist Sage.

Yet care is needed, for a tenet of the Taoist is that excess effort must be avoided, and that many present day evils are due to excessive tinkering. Lao Tsu recommended that the spontaneous flow of one's life should be followed, not diverted or forced. His Chapter 29 says, '. . . the world is a divine vessel: It cannot be shaped; nor can this be insisted upon. Anyone who shapes it damages it; anyone who insists upon shaping it, loses it.'

That having been said, we need to ask what modern psychology has to say about the Sage, and to do this we shall look at Abraham Maslow's study of the 'autonomous being', the fully-realized person.

MODERN PSYCHOLOGY

There have been attempts by psychologists to improve intelligence and to improve creativity, but none to improve wisdom – except possibly Maslow. He had difficulties in finding suitable models for study, and says,

> If we want to answer the question how tall can the human species grow, then obviously it is well to pick out the ones who are already tallest and study them. If we want to know how fast a human being can run, then it is no use to average out the speed of a 'good sample' of the population: it is far better to collect Olympic gold medal winners . . . The highest possibilities of human nature have practically always been underrated. Even when 'good specimens', the saints and sages and great leaders of history, have been available for study, the temptation too often has been to consider them not human but supernaturally endowed.[1]

This is true. Sages and other outstanding men and women have seldom been seen as models which it is to be expected that just anyone can copy. One has only to look at the other-worldly pictures that most people have of Jesus, St Teresa, the Lady Tara and the Buddha – all humans – to see the truth of this. Conversely, and incidentally, it is a mark of their singularity that such as Lao Tsu and Chuang Tsu are not often so imbued by lesser mortals with supernatural attributes. They come through at all times as very human. Perhaps this is because they dealt with, and still address, the everyday concerns of flesh and blood men and women, and did not appear to set impossible goals of behaviour and morality.

One of Maslow's basic ideas is that each of us has needs to be satisfied, and that these needs may be arranged in a hierarchy. At the bottom of the hierarchy is a layer of basic physical needs that must be satisfied before a person can transcend a basic animal-like existence. Such primary needs include food, shelter, sex, and warmth. 'Satisfaction' of these and higher needs implies the overcoming of driven behaviour in seeking their satisfaction, implies conscious control and the discovery of alternative means of reducing the need. The next higher level in the hierarchy is the need for companionship, love, and intellectual achievement, and so on up the hierarchy, each level further from the animal, and each needing to be transcended before it is possible to begin to satisfy the next. The whole process, according to Maslow, culminates in the emergence of the autonomous person. Where the normal person is content with the unconscious unplanned satisfaction of needs, the autonomous person takes steps to reduce those needs by a conscious change in personal values. Such values are universal rather than culture-bound.

What does it mean to be autonomous? It means to take control of one's life, and to be rid of those demands, almost amounting to irresistible inner commands, to conform to the wishes of others, and the expectations of one's culture. As Margaret Smith writes, fully autonomous people stay awake to all that is going on around them, and are pretty well in touch with their own interests and appetites. She says,

Looking at children gives us a good example of autonomy in action. Although most children encounter a lot of suppression from the complex cultural scene that we load upon them, the young child that is not too severely loaded with 'no's' will be pretty open about what he's doing and keen to express himself to you about it, and pretty direct in response to questions about his needs and preferences. He refers to his *actual knowledge of his needs* and replies quite straightforwardly.[2] (Original emphasis).

We shall see later in this chapter the way in which education, so-called, remakes children into socially-driven unbalanced beings, no longer able to express themselves spontaneously, autonomously, and happily.

Examples of autonomous beings, according to Maslow, included such as Martin Luther King, but were rare. While it is true that Sages are rare, they are not as rare as all that. Perhaps Maslow, a twentieth-century man, saw world notoriety as a criterion of self-realization. On the contrary, Lao Tsu and Chuang Tsu repeatedly said that worldly success or notoriety should be eschewed, that it was, indeed, a falling short of the goal.

They would have said that Maslow, in common with modern psychology, missed the mark.

Did they hit it themselves?

TAOIST PSYCHOLOGY

The aim of Taoist psychology is the same as much of modern psychology: to allow the individual to become free of driven, heteronomous behaviour. Ordinary, culture-bound values are to be abandoned. Yet the Sage lives in the world as it is. Sages are different in that they do not collaborate.

Given the complexities of life, a guide to living can never be straightforward. The classic guide, the *Tao Te Ching*, is certainly no exception. Like its fellow, the *I Ching*, it is enigmatic in the extreme and, especially in its original Chinese, open to a wealth of interpretation in translation. This in fact is as it should be: people have minds, and part of the process of maintaining balanced equilibrium is to use the mind to interpret life itself. Furthermore, 'quality of life', like enlightenment itself, is only to be known through each individual's own efforts, and thus cannot be communicated directly, but only either by example, or the wordless offer by a Buddha of a rose to a disciple, or through the enigmatic words of an oracle.

For instance, I interpret part of Chapter 52 of the *Tao Te Ching* as saying, '... the Sage still keeps to the Mother ... does not speak, does not perceive. That done, wisdom can never be exhausted. To do the opposite is to be no Sage.'

We can agree that much of our modern greed for amassing material things and increasing affairs is certainly due to the doors of perception being ever open. 'Keeping to the mother' we can see is a reference to the maintenance of balanced simplicity, childlikeness, and openness to the *yin*.

Chapter 22, more straightforwardly, says,

> Be humble, and you will remain entire.
> Be bent and you will remain straight.
> Be vacant and you will remain full.
> Be worn and you will remain new ...
> Because you do not compete;
> Therefore no one in the world can compete with you.

Being free of desires, either by good fortune or by self-discipline, frees one to move up Maslow's hierarchy.

Chuang Tsu emphasises the message of this chapter when he tells a story of a gnarled and bent old tree which is the only one saved from the woodchopper, because of its unattractiveness and unmarketability.

What psychological methods are employed by Taoists in achieving this unusual state of mind?

TAOIST PRACTICE

As Chapter 8 of the *Tao Te Ching* says,

> The highest goodness is like water.
> Water is beneficent to all things, but does not contend.
> It stays in places which others despise.
> Therefore it is near Tao.

Chuang Tsu, the happy Taoist philosopher, describes how Khiang, the master carver, went about making an item of furniture which in its finished perfection astounded all who saw it. Asked his secret, he described how he meditated, guarded his spirit and did not become distracted by trifles, forgot all thought of success, forgot his body and forgot all about the court that was waiting for his work. He described how his mind was emptied of all but the thought of the piece he was to make. Then he describes how he went into the forest and searched for and found the right tree, in which he could see the perfected piece of furniture. All he had to do was put out his hand and begin. 'My own thought met the potential of the wood, and from this natural meeting came the work you ascribe to magic.'

This is rather different from our own furniture makers stuffing sofas with toxic foam with a view to making a fast buck.

In the same way, Chuang Tsu describes the work of a master butcher who never once had to sharpen his blade in forty years, so skilfully did he see the joints in a carcase. If either of the men in the examples had come upon a difficulty, they would have considered themselves to have failed.

There is an innocence to the men that he describes, but it is not an ingenuous innocence. It is an acquired innocence, gained by long apprenticeship and painstaking work. As it is said in Zen, a mountain before working for enlightenment is a mountain, is something quite different when enlightenment is being worked for, and is once more a mountain when enlightenment has been achieved. In their own way, the woodcarver and the butcher were both Sages, both at the final stage of 'seeing the mountain.' Would either of these masteries, much less the path to their acquisition, be accorded worth in today's schoolroom, anywhere in the world? Only the strictest openness to rigorous measurement will enable anything taught today to qualify as of worth.

MODERN PRACTICE

Chuang Tsu compares such limpid masters as the wood worker and the butcher with more ordinary men, and what he says can apply equally to our own time: 'If an expert does not have some problem to vex him, he is unhappy! He feels that he is wasted, and casts about for a means by which to impress with his learning . . . Produce!' exhorts Chuang Tsu, tongue in cheek, 'Get results! Make money! Make friends! Make changes! Or you will die of despair!'[3]

And Chuang Tsu did not have an education system to contend with.

Once, men learned at the feet of masters as naturally as ducks take to water, or as any three-year-old child plays. Three-year-olds, seeing the mountain for the first time, have the same air of total absorption as Master Khiang displayed, and have the same lack of concern for anything outside the activity to hand. Young children learn by a process akin to osmosis, without stress or strain, all that they need to do in their environment and for their own development. It is likely that pre-industrial people do the same.

We, however, are post-industrial. Education, almost everywhere in the modern world, has taken a wrong turning. Industrial and post-industrial children have this ingenuous innocence driven out of them, and thus few, when grown-up, attain to the acquired innocence of the master craftsperson.

Production line methods have spread to education. Passive learning of the 'get your heads down and don't move till you've learnt it' variety is the resulting evil. It is evil because it goes against the grain of the natural child. Few modern educationists stand out against this trend. One that does is Paolo Freire in his *Pedagogy of the Oppressed* when he writes of modern methods turning the pupils into 'containers', into receptacles to be filled by the teacher. 'The more completely he fills the receptacles, the better teacher he is. The more meekly the receptacles permit themselves to be filled, the better students they are.'[4]

This non-organic instruction (not to be confused with education) is counter-productive in two ways, not because it fails to achieve its aims, limited as they are, but because it causes an attitude of mind that is hostile to education. In addition, it causes an alienation which was not apparent in the master craftsmen: they were at one with their environment in a creative relationship. Modern children are trained to see the world out there as a target for acquisition, not as a part of themselves. How else are they to join the consumer society?

True learning maintains a creatively playful relationship: the world out there and the world within are one, harmonious. The harmony remains when school is finished and so Master Khiangs have a chance to emerge.

Once upon a time, and not so long ago, a boy or a girl had a chance to sit by a river, or on a stone door step, and dream. Now life is stern and life is earnest, and not a moment is to be wasted. In any case, it is no longer safe for a child to sit by him- or herself by a stream or on a street corner. Rape and murder lie in wait there as the warped minds of the 'I want and I will have' consumers illustrate the actual results of present-day schooling.

Chapter 27 of the *Tao Te Ching* says:

> If the teacher is not respected, and the student not cared for,
> Confusion will arise, however clever one is.

It is not possible to be a teacher and to have a nine-to-five mentality: teaching is in the fullest sense of the word, a vocation. Now teaching is just another job, and it is the rare teacher who retains the respect that was once his or her due.

Neither are students cared for: the older the child, the more deeply they are initiated into the consumer society, the more alienated from wisdom – and learning – and school they become. The students are not cared for.

Indeed, children are cared for less and less, except in the lucky home, or if they are fortunate enough to meet a true teacher. In the main, however, the youngest of children are swiftly inducted into consumerism and habits of instant gratification. Schools are places in which the future citizen is prepared to take his or her place in the prevailing culture. Autonomy is not encouraged.

Chapter 48 of the *Tao Te Ching* says:

> In the pursuit of learning, every day something is acquired.
> In the pursuit of wisdom, every day, something is dropped.
> Less and less is done, until non-action is achieved.
> When nothing is done, nothing is left undone.

Just as the work of Master Khiang testified. In our age, what happens is that people from birth to old age and death are not valued unless they are acquiring, either goods or information. But of what use are acquisitions if their owner is not wise? 'What shall it profit a man if he gain the whole world, and lose his own soul?' 'Get results! Make money! Or you will die of despair!'

People are not seen now by their fellows as possessors of immortal souls – why should they, since God is dead? No longer joined by commonalty of any kind, is it little wonder that they become merely objects out there in the puzzling fantasy world of desires and their satisfactions?

Once the world has become peopled not by others just like me, but by projections of my own desires, little different from the flickering pictures on my television screen, then hell is readily let loose. Anything can become an object of desire, and since objects of desire are there for the desire to be satisfied, so I can treat others with a cool disregard for their humanity and a total regard for their value to me in the satisfaction of my desires. They are objects, not subjects, and I am alone in a world of my desire, and am myself an object to other subjective beings. I therefore fear them for what their desires might do to me. So one depersonalized object is disposed to be set against others, and the laws of nature are screwed up.

SUMMARY

'Others all have more than enough.' How is one to seek to avoid anxious disequilibrium when faced by the sight of one's neighbours and the whole world, it seems, busily seeking to amass riches? How to be contented? How to strive to reach the stage of development to which the humble Master Khiang had moved?

In the last chapter, we glanced doubtfully at the way of religion. In this chapter we have looked at two other ways, one ancient and one modern.

The distinction between the two is that the modern way, epitomized here in the psychology of Abraham Maslow, is primarily concerned with the objectification of humans, with turning them into objects of study, in which the individual is lost in a worthy study of autonomous behaviour in general. It contrasts with Taoism which seeks to address individual men and women in their private and subjective searches for autonomy, wisdom and long-term happiness.

The Taoist Sage, whether woodcarver or computer operator, seeks therefore to operate in harmony with the laws of nature, the study of which is a constant preoccupation.

The object of this gentle discipline is to return to the state of 'the uncarved block', and this requires above all an attainment and a mastery of stillness, combined with spontaneity of action when action is necessary. 'In repose the Sage shares the passivity of the *yin*, in action the energy of the *yang*.' Yet such a path demands that Maslow's lower needs have been satisfied.

What in theistic religions is an effortful obligation to conform to the will of God (and if God has gone and died, then the obligation is dead too) is in Taoism a natural co-operation with the harmony of the universe. Questions to do with sin or virtue do not enter the Sage's calculations. If such matters are thought about at all, sin is seen as ignorance or madness since contravention of the laws of nature brings inevitable punishment. Pure Taoism is not concerned with ethics or religious practice, creeds or dogma. Even though they became features of later Taoism, Lao Tsu and Chuang Tsu deplored hermitages and monastic orders: they would feel that Sages should be out and about in society, not interfering, but keeping their ideals ever-present and accessible to all their neighbours.

Pure Taoism is not a religion. Consequently the *Tao Te Ching* does not set out to point the way to a future heaven, and in only one chapter does it point back to an ideal Golden Age. It can be used as a guide to happiness and self-cultivation now, a guide to negotiating the shoals and rocks of the stream of this present life with equanimity. In this it is unlike those religious books which point to a future perfection of bliss after death. If it must be compared to a religion, Taoism is more often compared to Buddhism, with its approval of 'the Middle Way' as a path to follow in this life, and countless other lives.

But, unlike Buddhism, rigorous and tending to pessimism as it is, Taoism does not concern itself with innumerable future lives. Instead, it is more concerned with this one life and its perfection, looking to increasing this life's span even to immortality in this life in order to be able to do so.

Immortality is a much used and much misunderstood concept. To me, it seems clear: we possess immortality now, in this minute. I shall never experience death. How can I? If death is oblivion, I cannot experience that. If it is not oblivion, then existence continues, and again death is not an experience I shall have. To achieve this realization may be a kind of enlightenment, but is not cause for over-excitement.

What is a good quality of life? An answer will surely involve the ability to live harmoniously and autonomously with one's neighbour, with nature, with oneself — and one's neuroses.

Where other people are all *yang* or all *yin*, the Sage aims at harmonious balance. As Chapter 42 says, 'All things are backed by the Shade (*yin*) and faced by the light (*yang*), and harmonized by the immaterial breath (*ch'i*).'

What is being aimed at is autonomy: the ability to take control of one's life and one's desires in a happy relationship with neighbours near and far, human and non-human. Autonomy implies freedom from the dictatorship of collectivism and the freedom to be inner-directed rather than other-directed. Only when men and women attain to these freedoms more generally than now may wider change come about: a change that will alter the present situation in which hunger and poverty are the lot of more and more of our fellow human-beings: those neighbours who are being denied the satisfaction of the most primary of Maslow's hierarchy of needs.

This greening is the subject of my next chapter.

CHAPTER FOUR

Cherishing the Water Dragons

James Lovelock, in the Gaia hypothesis, puts forward the view that the Earth is a living organism that is kept alive by the health of the biosphere. Life in the form of living organisms, he claims, maintains the earth, rather than the other way about. The earth is to be cherished through care for animals and plants: 'To see the Earth as a living organism makes tangible the concept of stewardship and focuses our hearts and minds on what should be our main environmental concern.'[1]

Taoists go a little further. They believe that the earth, the cosmos, and all of creation spring from the *Tao*, the ground of all being. The *Tao* manifests itself in energy, *ch'i*, which flows through humans in the acupuncture meridians, and also in the earth in dragon veins. Not just the earth and its inhabitants, but the entire cosmos is one living breathing entity. We shall see in a later chapter how our bodily health depends upon our bodily *ch'i* being kept in balance. In this chapter, we see that our place in the world depends upon earthly and heavenly currents of *ch'i* being kept in harmony and balance. As conscious beings, we have a responsibility.

This chapter is about the ways in which we fail in our stewardship, and about ways in which ancient Taoism can improve modern matters.

THE PROBLEM

Taoism speaks sometimes of a golden age, as in the penultimate chapter of the *Tao Te Ching:*

Supposing there is a small state with few people.
Though there are various vessels I will not have them put in use.
I will make people regard death as a grave matter and not go far away.
[How seriously do we regard the road death statistics]?
Though they have boats and carriages they will not travel in them;
Though they have armour and weapons they will not show them.
I will let them restore the use of knotted cords [instead of writing].
They will be satisfied with their food;
Delighted in their dress;
Comfortable in their dwellings;
Happy with their customs.
Though the neighbouring states are within sight
And their cocks' crowing and dogs' barking within hearing;
The people (of the small state) will not go there all their lives.

DYNAMIC IMBALANCE

Lao Tsu paints an appealing picture that conjures up a vision of the lives of the hermits that John Blofeld met centuries later and whom he describes in his book, *Taoism: the Quest for Immortality:*

> Any number of different examples might be chosen to illustrate the Chinese feeling for natural beauty; but the most perfect expressions of that love were to be seen on the slopes of the holy mountains where Taoist hermitages clustered. Though generally remote and not very easily accessible on account of the distance from roads and railways, the hermitages were no longer simple cottages . . . Invariably the sites had been determined in accordance with the sacred science of *feng shui* . . . In their vicinity, moon-viewing pavilions hung above tremendous gorges filled with iridescent clouds of spray and echoing the muted thunder of the torrent far below.

Like any Utopia, Lao Tsu's seems impossible to attain, and the chapter is written, it seems, only to raise a sigh in the reader, and to give a sad realization that, even if it did exist, such a state is vulnerable to being gobbled up by greedy neighbours. Chuang Tsu describes this most accurately[2].

We now live on a planet and in an age in which overstretched *yang* forces appear to prevail with very little countervailing *yin*. Words like profit, agribusiness, solar windows and so on spring to mind: all effects of thrusting *yang*.

Neither Lao Tsu's nor John Blofeld's picture appear to offer much of practical value to us entrapped in our urban decay and polluted countrysides, our famines and our aerosol-cultures. Yet Taoism persists. In any extreme, there is the seed of its opposite (See Figure One).

There are greener shoots: Green Peace, The Green Party, Friends of the Earth. These movements are born of a *yin* reaction to over-strong *yang*. However, too often they appear to model themselves on what they oppose. Too many such organizations have the word 'Fight!' on their members' lips.

RURAL IMBALANCE

So fast is the attack on the environment in this, the latter end of the twentieth century of the Christian era, that any account of it must be out of date by the time a book about it is published. At the time of writing, a major concern is the depletion of the ozone layer. This is partly caused by the use of chlorofluorocarbons (CFCs) in aerosols and certain kinds of expanded polystyrene. Allied to this there are worries about the enormously damaging effect of the burning of equatorial forests. Whatever the cause, the effect of this depletion is to allow more ultraviolet rays to penetrate the earth's protective atmosphere, resulting in more skin cancers, reduced crop productivity, depleted fish stocks and climatic changes.

The interconnectedness of all creatures on earth implicit in Taoist cosmology (and the Gaia hypothesis) is brought out when we turn our attention to animals. One of the ways in which we manage to obliterate whole species of plants is, of course, in the wholesale deforestation of the tropical rain forests and in the production of Acid Rain which is another cause of the ruination of forests and the killing of fish in dead lakes. Apart from our reckless obliteration of whole species of visible animals and plants, there are countless species of microscopic creatures and plants that are disappearing for ever (one every half an hour according to Friends of the Earth in 1988), which in their going contribute to the general imbalance of nature. For example, it is said that certain microscopic marine plants are likely to be burnt up by the ultraviolet rays admitted by the depletion of the ozone layer. The plants manage, left to themselves, to modify the climate over the oceans in ways which ensure their own survival as a microscopic species. If they go, then such macroscopic phenomena as cloud formation, rainfall and sunshine reaching the surface are all likely to be affected, with consequent effects upon our own everyday comfort.

A cure, partial or complete, is in our own hands – but we may have to give up some of our creature comforts in order to achieve it. Again the question arises: are we mature enough to act to our own present (slight) disadvantage in order to secure the future for our children? Indebtedness of, for instance, Brazil to the developed nations is a cause of the reckless attack upon her rain-forests: unless developed nations are ready to suffer for the world, little can be expected in the way of a reversal of the trend.

Primitive hunter-gatherers were – and are – careful to preserve a balance between their needs and the needs of the countryside in which they lived. For long ages, this wise mentality persisted: the soil was treated with respect, and given a chance to recuperate by such means as crop rotation. Such farmers still carry on in their old ways, but the sounds of machinery come ever nearer.

No one should need much telling about the bad effects of agribusiness on environmental balance. Yet *yang* prevails unchecked, and deforestation, the grubbing of hedgerows, over-fertilization with its consequent pollution and soil destruction persist. Came the age of machinery, capitalist expansion and abstract money, and all contact with the soil was lost, at first in the cities, then in the country itself: everything was seen as there for the taking in order to make a big profit now, and to literal hell with the future.

URBAN IMBALANCE

The trend is not only rural.

A city is like a body, having its own metabolism. Given over-development, the city comes to resemble a cancerous growth, its cells multiplying in an uncontrolled manner. Urban planners become more like the antibodies in a cancerous tissue, fighting a hopelessly losing battle.

All developing nations create cities. These have the immediate effect of sucking in people from the rural areas, upon which the country could depend, causing overcrowding, and creating the conditions for disease, infant mortality and squalor. Cities of twenty million inhabitants are confidently predicted for the next century, while it becomes increasingly clear that such conur-bations cannot begin to service their populations in any proper way. For example, in Alexandria in 1988, four million people were served by a sewage system designed for one million. Yet desert nomads flock to such places.

FENG SHUI: DYNAMIC BALANCE

Meanwhile, satisfied with their food, delighted in their dress, comfortable in their dwellings, and happy with their customs, there are Taoist Sages.

The Taoist respect for dynamic balance in country, town, home and psyche is well illustrated in their science of geomancy, *feng shui*, literally 'wind and water'.

This science started in the Chinese concern with the placing of the graves of their ancestors: their site could be favourably placed or not, according to the state of the cosmic energy, *ch'i*, at the time of the burial. Experts in *feng shui* were employed to ensure that the grave was sited correctly, and that the burial took place at an auspicious time. They did this by using complicated instruments based on the magnetic compass, by the use of calendars and the client's birth signs.

The flow of *ch'i* in humans and environment was (and still is) believed to be detectable and controllable. In the body, the study resulted in acupuncture. In the landscape the currents were to be seen in the disposition of mountains, valleys, and water courses.

The latter were believed to be the most obvious flowlines of *ch'i*. Fast-flowing or straight-flowing water (often, in common with straight roads, canals, and railways, called 'secret arrows') was avoided, since it conducted *ch'i* away (and since water is symbolic of money, this was doubly unfortunate). Slow, sinuous courses, on the other hand, accumulated *ch'i*, especially if there was a pool.

Practitioners of *feng shui* were concerned not only with these 'water-dragons', living in streams and materializing in clouds, but with mountain-dragons. They looked in hills and mountains for dragon shapes and for evidence in the landscape of the Azure Dragon's mating with his consort, the White Tiger. The eastern heaven was the abode of the Azure Dragon, while the western was ruled by the White Tiger, and it was especially auspicious to find ranges of hills which conformed to the pattern which would be formed by their mating. '. . . . The greatest generation of *ch'i* occurs at the point where the loins of the dragon and the tiger are locked together in intercourse.'[3]

Such sites would be rare, and monopolized by the rich and powerful, so that poorer people could only be advised to avoid completely flat ground for burial sites. If necessary, and if possible, trees could be planted or mounds constructed. Predominantly *yin* (softly undulating) ground was placed in the sort of conjunction with *yang* (boldly rising) ground that would enable copulation to take place.

As has been hinted, *feng shui* practitioners extended their sphere of influence to this side of the grave, and were extensively employed in the placing of homes for the living. It is a common sight in rural parts of south China to see attempts to control *ch'i* by the artful placing of trees and the construction of pools.

Such experts are still extensively employed, even in places such as Hong Kong, or wherever Chinese have settled, in the siting and foundation-stone laying of office blocks and apartments. Big Chinese banks and business houses ensure that they have the *feng shui* reading to hand when new plans are in the making. In the same way, domestic architecture uses the science.

Feng shui practitioners believe that a house or room is like a body, having its own metabolism. Its occupants are its organs, to be nourished by a healthy and balanced flow of *ch'i*. This belief resulted in traditional houses being built around a central court, so that no matter how far from the country, the inhabitants were never out of touch with the elemental universe. For in the central courtyard they had a garden. Around this garden, the rooms faced inwards, turning the inhabitants away from the workaday world towards the ideal of simple nature.

So nature was enlisted in the search for a harmonious and happy life. Yet nature inculcated respect for balance: the workings of *yin* and *yang* were apparent, reminding men and women that they too were subject to their interplay, that they too were a part of what they created and enjoyed. Without human influence, the garden would not have existed. Without the garden, men and women would be cut from their roots, especially in the town or city.

Such awareness of and respect for the principle of dynamic balance has been lost in the west, and is only clinging on by its finger nails elsewhere. It is on its re-establishment that the future of Gaia depends. Considerable ingenuity will need to be generated to achieve this.

Just such ingenuity is exhibited by Chinese traditionalists living in cities in their efforts to maintain and foster the advantages of the *yin/yang* awareness associated with nature and gardens. Around them 'secret arrows' are built into the environment in the form of straight avenues, railway lines, telegraph lines and so on. The services of the *feng shui* practitioner in combating their effects are in increasing demand among those who can afford the fees, and do-it-yourself methods are increasingly used by those who cannot.

Furniture is placed so as not to obstruct the circular flow of *ch'i* from room to room: the placing of windows and doors should also encourage this. In practical terms, the occupants should be able to move from room to room without bumping into corners or furniture: if they can do this, so can the *ch'i*, which has been compared to a dancer who cannot perform well on a cluttered stage.

In urban areas, mirrors, 'the aspirin of *feng shui*', are essential. They can be used to reflect or deflect bad *ch'i*, preferably back to its source. In ancient days mirrors were worn on the body or the shield, acting as amulets. Nowadays they may be hung inside and outside houses, performing the same sort of function. They can be used to provide doors where none exist, or to widen rooms into better proportions.

In gardens, where they can be afforded, there will be rocks, miniature bonsai trees and, of course, water. Mountains, valleys, rivers and lakes will all be there, mimicking the greater world beyond. Perhaps some form of primitive magic is at play: control of the macro- by the micro-cosmic. In the same way, stones and pebbles are collected: those that possess characteristics of the larger world are much prized. There is an especially heavy reliance on the use of water, the home of the water dragon and the symbol of wealth and affluence. Flowing and still water symbolize respectively movement and repose, the complementary opposites of *yang* and *yin*, and water-worn stones symbolize the interaction of the soft and the hard. Everywhere in the well-planned garden *yin* and *yang* are to be seen.

How much the heavy hand of the machine and the profit motive will affect the use of this ancient science is not clear: it seems to be alive and well even yet among the hard-headed business community of the big Chinese cities. It is good to see that they are still concerned to pursue some sort of dynamic equilibrium in their hectic lives of business and their more tranquil lives at home. This in itself gives a picture of *yin* and *yang* alternating in the production of well-rounded human beings who, pursuing happiness in a balanced life-style, will preserve the Earth through their reverence for life and the flow of cosmic energy, *ch'i*.

It is difficult for us, living in the midst of it, to realize that mechanization, consumerism, agribusiness and the like have been around for a micro-second in terms of the history of the earth, and for a very short period in even the recorded history of humankind. It is to be hoped that irreparable damage is not done to prevent a return to balanced sanity and a respect for such a mystic representation of wisdom as *feng shui*.

THE *I CHING*

Another ancient representation of wisdom is the *I Ching*. An example of its use is again attempted here, resulting in something not very startling in its common sense, but startling in its appositeness. Interpretations are based on John Blofeld's text and the method again employed the use of three coins: the fall of a preponderance of heads being *yang* and of tails being *yin*. Three like heads represent a coming change in a line.

A question is put.

We confine ourselves to the problem of the nuclear power industry, and ask the question: Can the creation of electricity through the use of nuclear power be made safe for humankind?

Hexagram C

For the hexagram that emerges, see Hexagram C. This is Number 4, with moving lines 1 and 6 (which change the hexagram to Number 19), and is entitled 'Immaturity, Uncultivated Growth'.

The text reads:

Immaturity. Good fortune! I am not one to seek out uncultivated youths, but if such a youth seeks me out, I shall at first read out and explain to him the omens. Yet should he ask me many times, just because of his importunity, I shall not explain anything more. (The omen indicates) a need for proper direction.

The Commentary on the text reads:

Uncultivated growth! At the foot of the mountain lies a dangerous abyss. To abide where danger lurks is youthful folly. Yet such rashness may bring good fortune – fortune to be utilized when the moment comes . . .

The commentaries on the moving lines read:

for the bottom line: 'To enlighten immature youth, it is advisable to apply discipline; even fetters may be required, but to use them overmuch is harmful,' and for the top line: 'In dealing with youthful immaturity, there is nothing to be gained from doing what is wrong. Advantage lies in preventing wrong.'

Hexagram 19 is entitled 'Approach', and the text reads:

Approach. Sublime Success! Righteous persistence brings reward. However when the eighth month is reached, misfortune will befall.

Are these favourable or unfavourable responses? There is much comment by the *I Ching* on immature youths asking importunate questions. There is much talk of omens. Are Windscale, Three Mile Island, Chernobyl and all not omens enough, the *I Ching* is almost certainly asking? How often does immature humanity need to be told things in its self-created dangerous abyss? Perhaps a severe, but not fatal lesson needs to be taught.

If this occurs, (and Taoists must, as always, beware of wrong actions in the situation,) then sublime success will follow, though not last for ever.

So the next question (at the risk of importunity) must be: What should this Taoist do about nuclear power stations? (The answer occurs: write this book. Let's see.) For the hexagram that turns up, see Hexagram D.

Hexagram D

This is number 31, with moving line 2.
This is how the text reads:

Attraction. Sensation.
 Attraction, success! Righteous persistence brings reward. Taking a wife will result in good fortune.
 Attraction involves stimulation. The yielding is above, the firm below (the firm can easily support the weak). . . . the myriad objects owe their existence to the mutual stimulation subsisting between heaven and earth (a reference to yin/yang, marriage etc). Similarly the holy sage stimulates men's hearts and the whole world is henceforth at peace. The inner nature of everything in heaven and earth can be gauged by observing what it is that stimulates each of them . . .

(Interestingly, this is the same hexagram as emerged earlier in this book (p 16). Quite fortuitously, it illustrates the flexibility of the finite number of hexagrams to answer an infinite number of questions.)

'Moving line 2: Sensation in the legs – misfortune! Good fortune comes to those who do not venture forth.'

My interpretation of all this is that I should persist in what I am doing, stay at home and not take an active part in the world: no marches to Aldermaston for me. My business is to stimulate people's hearts. Taking a wife is a clear reference to the act of creation.

The moving lines moves the hexagram to Number 28:

> Excess. The ridgepole sags. It is favourable to have some goal in view. Success!
> Commentary: This hexagram indicates something altogether too large. The sagging ridgepole results from its weakness at both ends. . . . Nevertheless, the gentle and the joyful act as one, so it is good to have a goal in view; success will follow! The timely application of this hexagram is of vast importance.

So it seems I should not take on too much; I should be gentle and joyous and waste no time.

THE CONTRIBUTION OF TAOISM TODAY

Two practical applications of Taoism to saving the earth have been discussed. What is their importance in this day and age?

What has Taoism to offer that can in any way ameliorate the lot of us all? It is not now a philosophy of mass appeal, even in China, and certainly not in the West. Perhaps it never was.

There are no fast remedies that we can set in motion: fast foods are the death of us, instant cures have a way of giving birth to ever more horrible diseases.

It is, perhaps, too easy to look at the wisdom enshrined in *feng shui* and the *I Ching* and to say, comfortably, that a balance will be restored, even if the result of that dynamic equilibrium does not feature humankind.

It is easy to write sentences like: 'All that Taoism can do is to indicate the extreme probability of natural disaster restoring a balance in which we may or may not figure', and to indicate that we would do well to find a small state and live in it with our heads down, hoping the storm clouds may pass over without our getting too wet in the inevitable storm.

However, Taoism is not a world-negating philosophy of resignation: both *feng shui* and the *I Ching* demand human action. While Taoism teaches the gentle art of *wu wei* this does not imply the mindless flowing of a leaf in a stream, but intelligent participation in its flow.

Unwelcome change is almost always met with cries of 'Fight!' 'Fight the Motorway.' 'Fight for the Green Belt.' 'Unite and fight for your rights.' This is to oppose *yang* with *yang*, and not with *yin*. Instead of raising cash for banners and fly-posters, it could be used to present the encroaching authority with trees with which to embellish the motorway, to plant trees in the path of the motorway, to create a children's playground: in other words, to exercise reponsibilities rather than insist on rights. Much energy will thereby accrue rather than being dissipated, for the effort will gather strength from the forces in the cosmos that keep the dynamic tension within creative bounds.

Taoists have to detect and go with the cosmic flow: this is the alpha and omega of Taoism: to accept what is and seek to restore a balance; perhaps to examine, for instance, the forces that bring young people to the cities, and then to use the resulting insights as part of the move towards a saner and more balanced future.

Within every situation is the seed-pearl of change.

Somewhere the counterbalance is to be found, and somehow we have to ally ourselves with this balancing force. The Gaia hypothesis provides impetus: it fits in well with the beliefs of practitioners of *feng shui* that *ch'i*, the energy that informs all of life, flows throughout the earth maintaining the water dragons, humans, and animals. In our own way we too, if we are determined to follow the *Tao*, will play our part in maintaining the health of the biosphere, the realm of these water dragons.

If this is so, it behoves us to take a long hard look at what our leaders are doing, and this I shall do in the next chapter.

CHAPTER FIVE

Cooking Little Fishes

Change is inevitable. Change makes us uneasy and consequently much of our time is spent in trying to control change, either by creating it or by avoiding it. And yet as Chapter 29 of the classic *Tao Te Ching* says:

> The universe is sacred.
> You cannot improve it.
> If you try to change it, you will ruin it.
> If you try to hold it, you will lose it.

The way out of our uneasiness is to observe change, and to flow intelligently with it. This is *wu wei*, a process which can be likened to the skilful way in which a yachtsman uses the wind and the tide (both at times contrary) in order to reach port.

Instead of doing just that, most people place their lives in the hands of unskilful sailors, trusting to parents or lovers to make us eternally happy, or politicians to make the world a lastingly safe place.

POLITICS AND POLITICIANS

Why do people become politicians? For two reasons, perhaps. One is that they fulfill a need: as we have suggested, most people seek security, and will gladly delegate power to others who say they will provide it. The second is that there have always been men and women who have a psychological, often neurotic need to gain power, and who use that power to govern their fellow men and women. Their neurosis is one of deep insecurity: by

60

gaining power they hope to control change and increase their sense of security.

Politicians, therefore, aim to be masters or mistresses of controlling change. Few succeed, not only because of lack of skill but because few politicians are likely to admit to their neurosis, the results of which are summed up in the words of Emma Goldman.

> The State, every government whatever its form, character, or colour – be it absolute or constitutional, monarchy or republic, Fascist, Nazi or Bolshevik – is by its very nature conservative, static, intolerant of change and opposed to it.[1]

People are not, therefore, ruled by wise people (such show their wisdom by avoiding office). Instead, they are ruled by neurotic careerists who have little love for them, and whose main aim is to acquire the fruits of power, and to continue in power for as long as possible by resisting inevitable change.

Everything changes, but it seems that politicians react to this inevitable law of the cosmos with the same subtlety as the proverbial bull in the china shop. The ruled confirm them in their unsubtle actions by routinely confirming them in office. So politicians, big and small, good as well as bad, find power accruing, and need less excuse to administer power and devise more regulations and laws by means of which they hope to control the winds of change and preserve the status quo. But as the *Tao Te Ching* has it in Chapter 57:

> ... The more laws and restrictions there are
> The poorer people become ...
> The more rules and regulations,
> The more thieves and robbers.

THE TAOIST VIEW OF POLITICS

Change is inevitable, for its cessation is death. To maintain a dynamic balance in change, the wise politician is the one who governs as though cooking a small fish, very lightly. The most successful rulers, the most successful politicians, are those that make the least noise, and who rock fewest boats. (Unfortunately, in a modern democracy, such a person is unlikely to be adopted by a local party committee, and would probably not be seen or heard by the electorate.)

Just as hardheaded Chinese business people will not neglect the advice of geomancers, so wise political leaders will become aware of the flow of change and will, like yachtsmen, use its currents and eddies, its gales and calms to achieve their general aims. They will be wise to consult the *I Ching* in order to try to ensure that actions are made in accordance with the wind and tide prevailing.

That book, The Book of Changes, is full of good advice to those who have the ruling of their fellows thrust upon them, and also for those who, albeit misguidedly, actively seek high office. All are reminded that change is inevitable, that our petty human affairs are but a small part of the patterns of cosmic change, and that it is therefore prudent to be aware as far as possible of the direction of that change.

In the same way the ancient classic, the *Tao Te Ching*, the Book of the Way and its Power, is full of sound, if often unwelcome, advice to the politician: 'The more rules and regulations, the more thieves and robbers.' Yet politicians seek to preserve the status quo by devising laws.

But how can laws check change? How can human-made law emulate the subtlety and perfection of cosmic law? How can human law, for example, cater justly for individuals? As William Godwin has it,

There is no maxim more clear than this. Every case is a rule to itself. No action of any man was ever the same as any other action, had ever the same degree of utility or injury. It should seem to be the business of justice to distinguish the qualities of men and not, which has hitherto been the practice, to confound them. [Instead, he goes on to say, law-givers try to devise more and more laws aimed at covering every eventuality:] It is therefore perpetually

necessary to make new laws. These laws, in order to escape eva-
sion, are frequently tedious, minute and circumlocutory.[2]

Rules, by the very fact of their existence, will be broken: the
more laws there are, the more chances one has of being a
criminal if only by default. So their enforcement becomes ever
more difficult, and ever more important to the law-makers.
Penalties become more severe, and we read in Chapter 58:

> When the country is ruled with severity,
> The people are cunning.

In other words, the natives will become restive, a process of
balance will be set in motion, and the governed will seek to
outwit their masters. The immediate result will be more laws:
secret trials, fraud squads, neighbour encouraged to spy on
neighbour, the knocks in the night, and a general overreaching
by those in power. But the ruling clique cannot for ever stem
the flow of law-induced balancing rebelliousness. Overreaching
yang will lead to the inevitable rise of its opposite.

The ideal ruler, according to Lao Tsu, is one who acts on
the understanding that change is inevitable, that anything done
without first seeking the *Tao* is destined to have the most mar-
ginal effect on the world. Knowing this, they will in the first
place have been unwilling to seek office. When in office, they
remember to do as little as possible, to speak as little as possible,
to tread lightly and not force change: 'Peace and quiet are dear
to his heart . . .'

Yet it must be said that there have been Taoist rulers who
have been involved in wars. 'Light and dark coexist', and so
some Taoists have been involved in violent activity, for instance
in rebellion against tyrannical rulers. Lao Tsu realized that any
utopia would be only a part of the cycle, and not a static
millenarian state. He recognized that wars and rebellions were
a part of the cycle, for without them, peace would not exist.
The *yin* and the *yang* exist interdependently: without the one
the other would not exist. So there will always be men who

delight in killing, in domination, rapine and pillage, and those who oppose force with force.

The greater the one force, the greater the opposing complementary one. So everywhere throughout the *Tao Te Ching*, the emphasis is on the moderate application of opposites.

> Peace and quiet are dear to his heart,
> And victory no cause for rejoicing.
> If you rejoice in victory, then you delight in killing;
> If you delight in killing, you cannot fulfil yourself.
>
> (CHAPTER 31)

As Clausewitz said, 'War is a continuation of policy by other means,' and Lao Tsu continues his own theme into this, the ultimate political solution:

> A good soldier it not violent.
> A good fighter is not angry.
> A good winner is not vengeful. . . .
> This is known as the virtue of not striving.
> This is known as the ability to deal with people.
> This since ancient times has been known as the ultimate
>   unity with heaven.
>
> (CHAPTER 68)

A good soldier is not violent. He knows when to advance and when to withdraw; when to be strong and when to be weak.

> Yield and overcome. . . .
> Bend and be straight;
> Empty and be full;
> Wear out and be new;
> Have little and gain;
> Have much and be confused. . . .
> (CHAPTER 22)

Mao Tse Tung adopted this way of the Taoist warrior in his advice to his revolutionary army, constantly advising his officers to avoid confrontation, to lead the enemy into traps of their own making. 'The enemy advances, we retreat; the enemy camps, we harass; the enemy tires, we attack; the enemy retreats, we pursue.' 'Divide our forces to arouse the masses, concentrate our forces to deal with the enemy.'[3]

The *Tao* of politics seems clear.

> That which goes against the way of *Tao* comes to an early end . . .
> If the sage would guide the people, he must serve with humility.
> If he would lead them, he must follow behind . . .
>
> (CHAPTER 66)

As with a king, so with states:

> Therefore if a great country gives way to a smaller country,
> It will conquer the smaller country.
> And if a small country submits to a great country,
> It can conquer the great country.
> Therefore those who would conquer must yield,
> And those who conquer do so because they yield.
>
> (CHAPTER 61)

The wise ruler, then, will follow the principle of *wu wei* and the method of the judo fighter, giving way, yielding in order to overcome, avoiding head-on competition, remaining always a humble servant of the people. He avoids piling law on law and thus avoids the need for severe punishment and state violence.

Everywhere in the *Tao Te Ching* there is an emphasis on the humility which balances the doubtful pleasures of the glory that goes with office and power, and on the wisdom of avoiding contention and opposing like with like.

But such wisdom is not the *Tao* of average politicians in any age or land, who act as if they can change the laws of nature, and apparently believe that they are powerful enough to stop the universe in its majestic cyclic progression.

ANARCHISM AND TAOISM

Taoists have in the main recoiled in horror from any invitation to become part of the ruling establishment. Chuang Tzu, a great and wise interpreter and developer of Lao Tsu's ideas (he has been called Lao Tsu's St Paul) when asked to join government as a minister, asked rhetorically whether a turtle would be happier as a trophy on the palace wall or dragging its tail in the mud. He clearly regarded himself as a happy turtle dragging his tail in the mud, and refused the offer. Yet more is known of him than the powerful emperor that issued the invitation. He certainly can be said to have had more effect on the history of his country than any single emperor.

This and other stories indicate that there are undoubted similarities between anarchist theory and Taoism. Anarchism has had a bad press, so that it is interesting to note that there were strong anarchist principles applied in the drafting of the Constitution of the United States, and it is the Constitution that provides the brake on overweening political power on Capitol Hill. Other, older democracies are finding, to their loss, that they lack such a brake.

Anarchists are individualists, and are therefore opposed to the domination of any person by another, or of any group by another. At their best they are at least as moral a set of people as any other, having a deeply held respect for the rights of their fellows, and an inability to understand why anyone will willingly give to another fallible person or even more fallible group the right to direct their lives for the foreseeable future. Consequently they oppose coercion, even by the State's forces of law and order (which Alan Watts, that strange Western theologian, mocked in the phrase 'lawn order', bringing to mind all us worthy citizens mowing our safe suburban plots.)

Anarchists, at their best, organize their own affairs by aiming for consensus, and would organize wider affairs by means of consensus with other affiliated groups.

Taoist Sages, however, are not quite anarchists: they do not oppose government: they know that some men and women will

66

always seek to govern, and that most people will be content to be governed. Sages, instead, tend to withdraw from active involvement in politics, consistent with leading a good life: they will not actively campaign against government: they will weave their way through life, and the machinations of politicians, as skilfully as the old man who falls in a torrent and by adjusting himself to the currents emerges downstream unscathed before proceeding on his way.

A Sage will be sympathetic to a reduction in the power of rulers and an increase in the self-reliance and autonomy of ordinary people: a Sage could well agree with the principle behind Fred Woodworth's thinking, when he wrote,

> But the social principle of Anarchy is familiar and predictable also. Whenever one person helps another; whenever people solve their problems and no policeman or law instructs or compels – in short, at the taking place of any human development which is not mandated, ordained, decreed, controlled or interfered in by a legislature or by someone acting so as to force a result, we have the principle of Anarchy at work.[4]

Similarly, Taoists tend to regard any formal groups with wary suspicion, observing that organizational rules tend to stifle change and interfere with the free flow of *ch'i* between people. At the very least, they believe that organizations should aim to be ephemeral, dissolving when their immediate purpose has been achieved, a notion that is echoed in anarchist thinking.

> More radical, I think, is the conception that organizations be designed as impermanent, that is, actually be abolished at intervals. This idea of organizational impermanence ... originates from many considerations: (a) the idea that an organization be socially useful and that its members disband when it is no longer of utility; (b) the idea that organizations are often formed to solve particular problems and that they are no longer necessary when the problems have been resolved; (c) the idea that the rigidification of behaviour in an organization may be inescapable; and (d) the idea that over time people tend to identify organizational interests with their personal needs (and thus lose autonomy and authenticity).[5]

TAOISM AND THE BODY POLITIC

The British politician and statesman James Callaghan spoke of politics having a cycle of thirty years, after which time the political scene underwent a 'sea-change'. Sooner or later, he saw, checks and balances would come into play.

If a Sage, in a weak moment, should be prevailed upon to advise a politician, what sort of things would he or she say?

> Whenever you advise a ruler in the way of Tao,
> Counsel him not to use force to conquer the universe.
> For this would only cause resistance.
> Thorn bushes spring up wherever the army has passed.
> Lean years follow in the wake of a great war . . .
> Force is followed by loss of strength.
> This is not the way of Tao.
> That which goes against the way of Tao comes to an early end.
>
> (*Tao Te Ching*, CHAPTER 61)

No doubt the Sage would gently back up this quotation by pointing to the state of the country and of the world, at the accelerating rate of change, at the various opposing forces that are emerging from that change, and advise a careful study of the omens.

By this time the politician would be gone, and the Sage, unscathed and turtle-like, could wander off.

But, the people would say, this is not good enough: you promise us that a study of the *yin* and the *yang* can save us, or at least guide us towards survival.

To which the Sage might reply that all that can be done is to point out where a disregard of *yin* and *yang* is leading the people, and ask them to use their native wit and draw their own conclusions, remembering that the *yin* and *yang* is a universal force that will bring about its own checks and balances, whatever puny people may do. As Mao Tse Tung said, 'It is so with all opposites: in given conditions they are opposed to each other, and on the other they are interconnected, interpenetrating and interdependent . . .'[6]

Any effort of men and women that is made without consulting the omens will bring about change in ways that may be unwelcome to them. So the Taoist Sage would urge a study of the *Tao Te Ching*, in which Lao Tsu, that Sage of Sages who nowhere recommends a retirement from the field of human life, is concerned to see that we achieve the potential with which we were born: to follow the Tao, to be moral and to prosper.

If a modern political leader says that he or she is concerned for humanity and morality, and yet people are hungry and die before their time, then we are in the area of Orwellian newspeak: their actions belie their words, they are not for change. Lao Tsu was speaking (and, in a sense, still speaks) from the viewpoint of knowledge of the cosmos and its changes. He was a man, and he wrote his famous 5000 characters on the basis of what he saw going on in the world of his time, which remains our world.

What he wrote could be applied by today's statesmen and women.

The simple message is of humility, judo, of the reduction of the number of laws, and the belief that people, unpoliced, will be moral and that they will live in peace and gentleness with their neighbour. It requires no deep philosophic insight to argue that the fact that we are able to put forward the proposition implies that we have the relevant capacity.

But a capacity that is unused withers: by abdicating moral responsibility, we get the governments (and environments) we deserve. Taoists will say that it is up to each of us to be active in self-cultivation, and in our regard for that neighbour with whom we are one. Along with this will be quietude in external affairs if the fish is to be cooked, remembering at the same time that governments remain in power as the result of a process of checks and balances by the ruled, and that people who choose to allow a group or groups of fellow men to govern them and direct their lives need to be constantly vigilant.

Political decisions are being made all the time by the rulers of both rich and poor countries. Each of those decisions is bound to affect huge numbers of people: decisions about housing, about education and about the ways in which the distribution of wealth is managed. It seems that those people most directly affected are those who have the least power in the decision-making process.

Nevertheless, it is fundamental to Taoist belief that each of us is a part of what a Taoist Master, Ni, Hua Ching, has called a 'Universal Energy Net'. It follows from this that in our actions and thoughts we not only create our own life but directly and fundamentally affect the lives of others and the universe in general. The health of the body politic is therefore the responsibility of each one of us. If we shrug our shoulders and give power to fallible men and women, then we still bear responsibility for the consequences.

In the next part of the book, I leave behind doom and gloom (while recognizing that there are seeds of change in even the worst of circumstances). Instead, I look at ways in which the union of the Azure Dragon and the White Tiger can more clearly be seen to be having beneficial effects.

PART THREE

HOPE

Where there is no hope, there can be no endeavour
SAMUEL JOHNSON

CHAPTER SIX

The Rainbow Bridge

It is in its insights into the sources of creativity that Western thought comes closest to Eastern. In Taoist thought, creativity is seen to depend for its special qualities on the interplay of *yin* and *yang* as they seek to maintain balance in the streaming forth of the energy of the *Tao*.

It is a theme of this chapter that this happens more often and more surely in the Eastern arts than in those of the West, for artists of the East are culturally more aware of this importance of cosmic balance, of fullness and emptiness, than those of the West. It is in the balance achieved in the filling of emptiness provided by the artist, in the achievement of psychological closure, that insight is achieved by the observer.

We begin by considering a poem:

> Mount Lu in misty rain; the river Che at high tide;
> When I had not been there, no rest from the pain of longing.
> I went there and returned . . . it was nothing special –
> Mount Lu in misty rain; the river Che at high tide.

There is in this fragment an emptiness that we are impelled to fill. In Western terms, there is need for a gestalt-like closure. Just as a window depends on a blank space for its existence, so emptiness completes the poem.

Lao Tsu tells us in the *Tao Te Ching*:

> Thirty spokes unite at the wheel's hub:
> It is the centre hole makes it useful.
> Shape clay into a vessel;
> It is the space within that makes it useful.

73

> Cut out the doors and windows for a room;
> It is the holes which make it useful.
> Therefore profit comes from what is there;
> Usefulness from what is not there.
>
> (CHAPTER 11)

The vacant spaces are the *yin* aspect of creation, dynamically balancing the more obvious *yang* aspects. In the poem, apart from the obvious 'it was nothing special', the enclosing of the two middle lines by the identical outer lines somehow contrives to convert the centre into nothingness, a blank space in which nothing at all has apparently happened. But the poet has managed to create a wealth of potentiality for insight in those two empty middle lines.

The everyday world – the world of 'the ten thousand things' – does not stand still: it is in constant movement: changing and streaming in time. To fix it like some butterfly on a board seems on the face of it to be a contradiction. Yet somehow Taoist poets contrive to convey that streaming, and to maintain those tensions. Thus they manage to convey a realization of movement, and the hearer becomes a participant with the artist in this insightful pull towards the future.

GESTALT PSYCHOLOGY AND TAOIST CREATIVITY

The eye seeks to close gaps in incomplete figures (see figure 3). Gestalt psychology is based on this human propensity for seeking meaningful wholes. The emptiness in the centre of the poem is filled. It is filled from the resources of the reader: there are no aids provided by the poet, yet closure is achieved, the whole is resonant with meaning and there is subjective satisfaction. It is so in all good Taoist creative art, all of which is based on the

Figure 3. *An assortment of meaningless lines and angles, when re-arranged, suddenly acquire meaning.*

tension that exists between positive and negative, full and empty, light and shade.

Elizabeth Smith in her book *Choose Happiness* describes how, when studying Gestalt therapy, she 'began to gain . . . a new understanding of an organism's ability to regain a lost, natural wholeness . . .'

This is as good a description of people's need to regain the lost *Tao* as any, and it is in giving the audience opportunities to taste the *Tao* in achieving natural wholeness from disparate parts that the Taoist artists serve their fellow creatures.

The whole is something more than the sum of the separate parts, as can be seen not only from the fragment of poem, but in all Taoist creativity. There is a constant effort to achieve wholeness through the resolution of opposites.

It is in this that Western art is different from Eastern. All too often, the Westerner is presented with a complete whole to be admired for its craftsmanship and vision. But such works do little for the recipient: there is less tension to be resolved, less closure to be achieved, less intimations of cosmic wholeness, and less peace in the viewing.

THE STILL CENTRE

Indeed, a mark of much Taoist creative work is its peace. This is hardly surprising, since so much of it is to do with achieving a balance between opposites, leading to the satisfaction of closure. This peace is itself a balance of *yin* and *yang*, being achieved through *wu wei* on the one hand, and a mastery of technique on the other.

As to *wu-wei*:

> Tao abides in non-action
> Yet nothing is left undone.
> (CHAPTER 37)

Such a man or woman who attains to mastering *wu wei* is the one who, through the use of light and shade, weight and ethereality, fullness and emptiness, also masters the harmony of their balance.

Such mastery is nevertheless not achieved without disciplined effort. Mastery of technique, training of the eye and ear and such like, are all the result of much preliminary effort and discipline. This is the *yang* of the process, without which the non-doing, intuitive *yin* input could not be expressed.

Creation is not a process to be achieved easily: a mastery of technique is as important as a mastery of *wu wei* if spontaneity is to be achieved. It is through their dynamic equilibrium that the effortlessness of the finished work arises.

SPONTANEITY

An artist, whether from east or west, is freed to a great extent from convention, and is encouraged to be spontaneous. We find often in this book that the mark of a fully realized Taoist Sage is this very spontaneity. The Sage as an artist will not be afraid to discover and use idiosyncratic methods in order to touch the creative springes within. Watts describes the method used by a certain Ch'en Jung who, when drunk, encouraged *yin* by splashing ink on his pictures to make clouds, spat water out of his mouth to make mists, shouted, seized his hat and smeared his drawing with it. Afterwards, when sober, he finished his work off in a proper manner by using a brush (*yang*).[1]

Spontaneity and unconventionality are the hallmarks of Taoism and, often, of artists from East and West, in whatever medium their work is expressed. However it is arrived at, the harmony of the *yin* and the *yang* is the ideal to be achieved. Since Taoists, and by their influence Chinese artists in general, have the schema of the *yin* and the *yang* as part of their culture and psychology, they are more readily placed to incorporate them into their work.

While greater Western artists do arrive at such harmony (they have discovered the key to the gate that guards the bridge), inferior ones do not. Because of this learned knowledge, in which they have been immersed since birth, the run of the mill scribblers, painters and dramatists of the East are more likely to achieve artistic and creative integrity than their Western counterparts.

THE RAINBOW BRIDGE

There is a physiological basis for the creative power found in the juxtaposition of opposites. The unifying force of *yin/yang* has an organ within the human brain that will lead to the unity expressive of the Tao.

Physically, the brain can be seen to consist of two halves, two hemispheres. Through experimentation, it has been shown that the left hemisphere has to do with rational and logical thought, while the right has to do with the intuitive. They represent within the brain *yang* and *yin*, the Azure Dragon and White Tiger of artistic endeavour.

Creativity springs from their mating: to be totally in the intuitive *yin* mode would mean that one would not be able to communicate insights in any way logically, in any way to appear sensible to the audience. To be, on the other hand, operating totally in the rational mode would mean that intuitive insights were denied entry. There has to be a bridge between the two halves of the brain if the creative mind is to be given full expression. Is this bridge a figurative invention of the right hemisphere, or does it exist in reality?

It appears that it does. There exists in the skull what is called variously, depending from which hemisphere it is approached, either the *corpus callosum* or the Rainbow Bridge. Physically this link consists of a thick bundle of nerve fibres which run between the two sides of the neo-cortex. Psychically as well as physically, it appears to lie in the area that has been identified by mystics as the site of 'the third eye'.

The artist and the individual member of the audience both possess the two hemispheres and the rainbow bridge between them. The artist who wishes to communicate (and which artist does not?) has to use skill in leading the audience to share the same view from the bridge.

A painting can be examined coolly and dispassionately in looking at the use, for example, of perspective and the Golden Mean. Poetry has metre. In both, these and other technicalities do something more than satisfy the left hemisphere; they affect the right as well.

Symbolism and the use of archetypes, on the other hand, speak to the right hemisphere, but may also be appreciated from the logical side.

How the creative artist walks with the viewer hand in hand across the Rainbow Bridge is thus a matter of great skill. How it is done is culture-bound, but only to a limited extent: symbols and perhaps archetypes may differ between cultures, but the psychological need for dynamic balance between *yin* and *yang* is probably innate and universal, a ready-made tool for the communicating artist to employ.

The Chinese artist has the confidence to trust the audience to be participants in the act of creation: he or she will need to explain less, and may take one's hand on the Rainbow Bridge more often and more definitely.

YIN AND YANG IN TAOIST CREATIVITY

The Taoist, because of familiarity with the concept of yin and yang, already possesses a key to the Rainbow Bridge. It is a key that western artists might fruitfully use.

Taoist artists have a head start: they are aware of the *yin/yang* complementarity of the many aspects of creativity – including inspiration and technique – that have to be brought into a process of dynamic equilibrium in the production of the finished work.

Working within the distinctive Chinese culture, *yang* and *yin* are symbolized by the Taoist visual artist in a variety of ways.

Yang, for example, is symbolized by stallions, dragons, rams, cocks, horned beasts, mountains, jade, summer, and the south.

Yin is represented by such as fungus, whirling shapes of cloud and water valleys, the north, vases, peaches, female dragons, the peony, fishes, and chrysanthemums.

By placing such opposites in juxtaposition, Taoist artists intend that each should influence and balance the other and contribute to restful harmony in the eye and mind of the beholder on his or her own Bridge. This juxtaposition is insufficient in itself: there has also to be an element of the sort of tension that exists in change (and on bridges). The world of the ten thousand things does not stand still: it is in constant movement, constantly changing, ever streaming, like growing bamboos, rearing mountains, and mountain streams.

How is the tension achieved? In the poem, it is achieved, perhaps, by the phrase 'pain of longing', by the picture of the artist coming and going. How is it achieved in other art forms?

Painting

Chang Chung-yuan draws on a number of authors to illustrate the secret. 'Generally speaking, when the left side is vacant, the right side should be solid . . .'

'White vacancy is yang, solid ink wash is yin, darkness.'

This use of heavy and light, solid and vacant, in the proper hands, will fill the picture with vitality: the tension between them will cause the entire picture to be full of rhythm, of liveliness. 'Through that which is vacant the solid is moved, and that which is solid becomes vacant.'[2]

To fix such lively tension on paper or silk seems to be a contradiction. Yet Taoist artists manage to maintain tension and thus give birth to the satisfaction of closure and balance.

It is the brush, using watery ink on silk or porous paper that helps the painter or calligrapher to achieve this. Indeed, the use of such media forces the artist towards an immediacy that induces tension because of the possibility of irreparable disaster. As Alan Watts says, in discussing the art of calligraphy. 'If you hesitate, hold the brush too long in one place, or hurry, or try to correct what you have written, the blemishes are all too obvious. But if you write well there is at the same time the sensation that the work is happening on its own, that the brush is writing all by itself − as a river, by following the line of least resistance, makes elegant curves.'[3] There is immediacy: like life itself, there is a sense on which choices, once made, are irrevocable within the matrix of universal change.

Drama

There is a tension to *Macbeth* performed on a bare stage that is often lacking in traditional presentations. The beauty and clarity of Shakespeare's text is *yang*-like in its strength. This is balanced by the negative effect of the bare stage: the audience is encouraged towards the equilibrium of psychological closure. This effect is that which has long been achieved in traditional Chinese opera, in which the almost bare stage is left to be furnished by the imaginations of the individual members of the audience.

Sculpture

Oddly, sculpture shares with calligraphy the possibility of irreparable disaster in its execution: it is this quality that gives movement to the heaviest material, properly handled.

In the west, of all modern sculptors, perhaps Henry Moore and Giacometti approach closest to the balance aimed at by Chinese artists in other fields. Moore's heavy figures yet have a lightness when viewed against the sky; his use of solidity and space achieves the aim of balance. Giacometti, in his very different way, seems also to arrive at the same pleasing result: his curiously elongated figures balance in their elongation the heaviness of the material of which they are formed.

Both sculptors convey a sense of spontaneity: there is a sense in which their sculptures may be said to be growing from the ground or from their setting wherever the latter may be – a true mark of their genius.

Chinese sculpture and pottery themselves, however, are quite different. They rely on the discovery within the material itself of dragon shapes, swirling cloud shapes, and the like: attempts to fix in stone and clay what are of their very nature not to be fixed, in much the same way as Chinese painters fix clouds on silk.

CONCLUSION

Eastern traditional art seldom leaves the audience out on any kind of unbalanced limb: the juxtaposition of good and evil, dark and shade, heaviness and lightness almost always heightens awareness of an underlying harmony and encourages gestalt closure. Such heightened awareness is achieved without stress and strain, arising as naturally as a wave striking a shore.

At first glance, very much more appears to be demanded of

the audience of a western work of art than of a Chinese work. There is so much more analysis to be done, so much balancing, so much intellectualization. Modern Western works, in particular, are so much more clever and need so much more consideration. As a result, works of modern western abstractionists seldom have the fascination for Western eyes that Taoist works may have. In those eyes there appears to be a puzzled recognition of strong forces at play in a work which is both seemingly strangely stripped bare of detail and yet is satisfyingly complete.

> Heaven does nothing: its non-doing is its serenity.
> Earth does nothing: its non-doing is its rest.
> From the union of these two non-doings
> All actions proceed.

The energy of the Tao is constantly emerging, streaming forth towards the future, subject eternally to positive and negative polarities: as an aspect of nature, this cannot be ignored. Change is the primary fact of the manifest universe, and is achieved through a series of dynamic equilibria: Taoism believes that any artistic expression that ignores the fact has failed. The Taoist artist is concerned to achieve balance in his or her own mind, spirit, and work, and with making it more possible to achieve in the mind and spirit of the perceiver.

Chinese art is more readily accepted in the West than Chinese medicine, *feng shui*, and the like. This is no doubt partly due to the fact that art is a universal preoccupation, partly that it is is 'non-serious', but more likely still it is accepted because it satisfies universally human psychological and aesthetic needs. It forms, in itself, a safe bridge between the world hemispheres.

Similarly, in the next chapter, I shall show how a coming together of East and West is apparent in people's searches for security in the physical world of science.

CHAPTER SEVEN

Black Holes and Magic

According to Einstein[1], 'Science is the attempt to make the chaotic diversity of our sense-experience correspond to a logically uniform system of thought.' The words 'chaotic diversity of our sense-experience' are clear enough. It is not clear just what comes within the remit of scientific enquiry, and what is left outside, however, for there are logically uniform systems of thought that Western science seeks to disown.

THE LIMITS OF SCIENCE

Can anything that we experience be excluded as beneath the purview of science? In Emerson's[2] view, 'Tis a short sight to limit our faith in laws to those of gravity, of chemistry, of botany, and so forth.' What of art, meditation, mysticism and religion, to name only four other great pursuits of humankind? These consist of systematized forms of knowledge, each having its own general principles.

In this chapter I will look at science and also at magic, a parallel and related path by which we move towards understanding and control of the everyday world. Such a pursuit is still believed in and practised by the majority of earth's inhabitants – including those of the sophisticated West – as they seek systematized knowledge of those forces that affect their lives. Is that knowledge to be denied recognition and worth?

Louis Kronenberger[3] said, 'Nominally a great age of scientific enquiry, ours has actually become an age of superstition about the infallibility of science, of almost mystical faith in its non-mystical methods . . .' And, we could add, an age which still exhibits closed minds to many other recognized means of understanding the chaotic diversity around us.

Chambers Dictionary defines science as 'knowledge ascertained by observation and experiment, critically tested, systematized and brought under general principles: a department or branch of such knowledge or study: etc. From Lat *scientere* from *scire*, to know.' That being so, what then are the boundaries of science?

In the larger sense, and without distorting the words of the chosen definition, much more than what is generally accepted as worthy of scientific enquiry could be included. Science as generally accepted limits itself by its insistence on 'critical testing', by which is meant the ability to replicate and quantify circumstances and situations. But there are many fields of human enquiry, including many sciences, where this is neither possible nor desirable. These would certainly include such seemingly non-scientific aspects of human experience as the occult and magic. Included would certainly be Taoist magical medicine in the use of talismans, and possibly in its practice of acupuncture with its use of bodily channels (meridians) that are not detectable by scientific observation.

I am arguing that magic is a kind of science because it deals with the observation and systematization of observable phenomena, and, like western science, seeks for the ability to control.

Taoists have developed logically uniform systems of thought as a result of observation and experiment. That their observations are expressed in terms of cyclic change and *ying/yang* balance in no way invalidates them. For we see that such schemata can be shown to be satisfactory means of explanation and practical activity in a search for health, happiness, and some control of destiny.

To make sense of the world: that has been the story of intellectual endeavour.

The science which we in the West nowadays use in order to go about it has been a method characteristic of only a very small section of the world's population during a very short period of recorded history.

NEMESIS

The evidence is that modern scientific method has been, by and large, a mistaken effort, adding little to the sum of human happiness, and little or nothing to understanding the reasons for human existence and similar large questions that continue to exercise our minds.

We have developed a host of tools and techniques to improve our material lives, we have made immense leaps in our mastery of technology and our ability to master the external environment. We drive cars and space-craft, use solar power, harness waves and wind and communicate over vast distances by bouncing messages off vehicles in space. We produce theories to account for the creation of the universe, and seek to integrate our knowledge of the forces of nature from elementary particles to interstellar gravity.

Where is the parallel investment of time and resources in developing our inner worlds? How successful have we been in creating, in the generality of human beings, health, happiness and harmony? How successful have we been in eliminating hunger and poverty?

Science, as we understand it, is a latecomer to the story of humanity's efforts to come to grips with the sometimes frightening unknowns of our world.

Much of what is going wrong with the world today can be laid fairly, squarely and indubitably at the door of those people – ourselves – who have adopted the unbalanced view espoused by western science that creation exists for our benefit and manipulation. Western applied scientists are aggressive: they have to be, when their paymasters are breathing aggressively down their necks for fast results, within the lifetime of an elected government if possible. The result is that present-day science in the developed world too often goes against the grain of nature, and not with it.

Taoist, and Eastern philosophies in general, without exception take the view that such plundering affects the whole; that we are not separate from nature when we do things to it, extract things from it: we are doing it to ourselves. We are an integral part of nature: everything we do we do to ourselves.

How would the Taoist scientist/magician view the terrible things that we are doing to our spaceship planet in this modern age? They would be opposed to the growth of agribusiness: seeing in this an example of almost everything that is going wrong. They would laugh outright (or cry) at the butter and wheat mountains, the wine lakes obscenely spreading in the presence of the starving. They would know, fortunately for their sanity, that such obscenities are temporary, and the pendulum will swing once more towards sanity, but they will continue to weep for the dead child-victims of western idiocy.

They will shake their heads at the unbalanced idiocy of stock-piling nuclear and conventional arms, remembering some of Lao Tsu's aphorisms on the subject: 'The weakest things in the world can overmatch the strongest things in the world,' 'the best soldier is not soldierly,' 'the best conqueror does not take part in war,' and so on. The *yin/yang* tension in the present global arms situation they may feel can only be resolved either by the use and consequent dissipation of the weapons, or for the whole human race to come to its senses.

It seems that the whole world has been taken over by western notions of what constitutes science, and that the world is rapidly being destroyed by that lop-sided, unbalanced activity. What kind of science is it that cannot see beyond the carrot in front of its own nose?

Long term research is often under-funded, while short term research, too often directed at means of mutual destruction or financial competition, is funded generously. This lopsidedness will become more common as Western powers become poorer, exhausted by their own greed and aggressiveness to maintain 'standards' – a nice example of increasing *yang* tending to its own demise. It is the fallible human beings who head the super-powers who now have the immediate future of the human race and of planetary life in general in their hands.

The fear is that the lopsidedness will be corrected, that a sudden and, from the human point of view, cataclysmic dynamic balance will be achieved. As a correspondent wrote to the *Guardian*: 'The human race has developed technology to the point where it is posing all kinds of dilemmas for our choice and execution of existential priorities and moral judgements . . . It may seem callous to state it, but not everyone is supposed to survive. Either we accept and adapt to that as a painful but necessary truth, or it will be imposed upon us in some form of iatrogenic catastrophe, in the furtherance of planetary – and indeed cosmic – balance.'[4]

That is the fear.

TAOIST SCIENCE

Taoist science has a long pedigree, and a tradition of harmlessness and respect for that which it studies and uses.

Taoists are humble: they always have been, seeing themselves as they do as minute in the scale of the cosmos, and yet at the same time hugely responsible for the well-being of that cosmos. Their science is based primarily upon the observation and control of energy and its changes. The energy manifests itself as *ch'i*, and its changes are kept in balance by the meshing of the *yin* and *yang*. It is humankind's part in the scheme of things to help to maintain that balance.

Taoist science is therefore not far removed from the everyday concerns of ordinary people. The Chinese are nothing if they are not practical and down-to-earth, and philosophical insights into the nature of change are interpreted for the man and woman in the street in practical technology. In health and geomancy, to take but two examples, they have developed technologies that are firmly based on an underlying theoretical framework to do with maintaining a balance in the flow of cosmic power in humans and their environment.

For instance, they use needles in acupuncture to balance the bodily flow of *ch'i* in order to maintain health. They developed the *lo-pan* compass to detect the flow of beneficent *ch'i* in the earth in order to protect individuals and groups. Continual experiment and practical use over the centuries have led to great confidence in the methods, and some of such confidence is slowly spreading to the West.

In the field of medicine, for instance – to be looked at in more detail in the next chapter – if the end result is health, there is little difference to the patient between the use of a Taoist talisman, an acupuncture meridian, or a placebo pill.

Whether it be called magic or science – after all, it has been said that magic is in fact 'science in the tentative stage' – it is clear that the aim is to control change, and even in modern terms this is a very respectable scientific pursuit. The proof of any pudding is surely ultimately in the eating. A Taoist scientist does what a western scientist aims to do: to study and control the forces, internal and external, that affect the happiness and well-being of human beings. The difference is that the former has a respect for the whole of creation, and recognizes that a balanced approach is necessary, whereas the latter has an arrogant belief that ham-fisted imbalance can be corrected by main force.

Jung called us 'the unfinished being'. We in the West are certainly incomplete, for we spend too much psychic energy in countering the results of cutting ourselves off from the inbuilt homeostasis of nature.

A MEETING OF MINDS

Quantum Physics

If we look beyond the electron microscope to the smallest imagined wave/particle hypothesized by Western physicists, we find ourselves completing what has the appearance of a cycle, and approaching again the world-view of the ancients as expressed in Hindu, Buddhist and Taoist cosmology. Behind the tensions of the *yin* and the *yang* is the quantum field of the *Tao*. In Capra's[5] words, 'the quantum field, waving and vibrating, rhythmically alternating like the yin and the yang, forms things and dissolves them.' He explicitly likens the quantum field to the *Tao* with its energy, *ch'i*, constantly being balanced by positive and negative forces and tendencies.

Artificial Intelligence

A further breakthrough along the Rainbow Bridge between East and West may be found in the study of Artificial Intelligence. In this, very much work is being done in exploring at the theoretical as well as the practical level the connection between the physical aspects of the human brain, and their results as they appear in the mind (whatever and wherever that may be).

Already sentences like this are appearing: 'So if our idea of the physical ever expands to include mental phenomena, it will have to assign them an objective character – whether or not this is done by analysing them in terms of other phenomena already regarded as physical. *It seems to me more likely, however, that mental-physical relations will eventually be expressed in a theory whose fundamental terms cannot be placed clearly in either category.*'[6] The sentence I have emphasized appears to me to be bordering closely upon the wave/particle curiosity of quantum physics. As Heisenberg pointed out, it is not possible accurately to define simultaneously both the position and the momentum of an electron. Perhaps we are here witnessing another aspect of the *yin/yang* dichotomy detectable in physics in an essential feature of our minds. All opposites partake of the character of the *yin* and the *yang*. The observer of the wave/particle has to perform a mental balancing act to arrive at some sort of dynamic equilibrium. So also may the observer/experiencer of the mind/-body curiosity.

Jung

A long established thinker who has brought the two world hemispheres closer, and who did it much more knowingly and deliberately, was Carl Jung. I want in this chapter to mention two of his ideas.

The first is the theory of the collective unconscious, involving the concept that all human minds share racial memories of myths and archetypes.

His ideas pushed him to the limits of scientific respectability, yet his ideas have a habit of cropping up years after he first wrote of them, and none more so than this one. It was opposed to the ideas of the time, dominated as they were by the individual psychologic theories of such as Sigmund Freud and the neo-Freudians on the one hand and 'hard' scientists on the other. Psychology was seen as to do with observing the isolated individual, as though pinned beneath a microscrope, and as having nothing to do with racial history and little to do with humans as social creatures. But it is clear that individuals are not in fact discrete beings: they are what they are only in terms of their total space/time environment. Jung's influence is growing, now that science is beginning to throw up ideas that indicate that the mythic and mystical may be about to become respectable again.

The other of Jung's interests was to do with coincidence and synchronicity.

At the time, this study was placed on a par with the rest of the old man's interests, which were in general right against the grain of accepted science, concerned as it was with a limited area of our experience, namely with cause and effect and what could be observed and measured. In Jung's theory of synchronicity, as in the collective unconscious, there was an element of the mysterious, of the mythic, of, dare it be said, the occult, which put it right outside the pale of scientific respectability.

His concept of synchronicity arose from observations he made, particularly in his clinical work. An oft-cited example is of the occasion when a patient was telling him of a dream in which an Egyptian Golden Scarab figured. As the patient related the story of the dream, Jung became aware of a knocking on the window. Investigating, he found the knocking was being caused by a beetle which, he found, was the nearest European relation to the Egyptian Golden Scarab. Its appearance was clinically useful at the time, but more important it was just one of a number of such observations which Jung believed went beyond the merely coincidental. Hidden in them were significances that went beyond the merely rational to the underlying meaning of situations.

He believed that he had detected the operation of what he called an 'acausal connecting principle'. In such occurences, two events could be connected by more meaning than there was any right to expect using logical, linear, left brained thought. He believed there was a connection between such synchronistic events and the workings of the collective unconscious.

It is interesting that Jung's friend, the physicist Pauli, believed that many parapsychological phenomena, including apparent coincidences, were visible traces of an underlying connective principle in the universe.

In the collective unconscious, the whole of the recorded history of mankind is of a piece, and its experience draws all of us together as sharers in the historic and mythic past. Synchronicity appears to draw all people and objects, living and dead, material and non-material, together as participants in one another.

CONCLUSION

All these lines of thought serve to underline John Donne's 'No Man is an Island . . .' It is now being increasingly realized by many, including an increasing number of hardnosed scientists, that this poetic insight is indeed true, even if only from the increasingly respectable realization that the observing subject can affect the observed object at all levels, that no atom or wave/particle is an island entire of itself, but that all of these, from psion to galaxy, are all the time and in every respect totally dependent on the others.

The Western scientist is beginning to find that we are more than a biological machine, even as we are less than a spiritual angel. The mechanics of our brain produce more than straight answers, statements, and equations: it produces, in a way that we find baffling, poetry and intuitions that are equally valid.

Scientists are exploring inner space: they are also exploring outer space, going beyond the nearer reaches of our solar system, exploring really deep space with instruments that pick up radiations that set off through the universe before we appeared on our planet. Will they find out what happened *before* the Big Bang? Chinese Taoists have held that all of creation, 'the ten thousand things', emerges from the Tao and returns to it. If they accept the Big Bang theory, they would therefore see it in terms of one of a succession of Big Bangs. Western scientists seldom go beyond the second preceding the Big Bang: to them the second before is *terra incognita*, in which lurk monsters too terrible to behold, perhaps.

Yet there are some who venture out along the Rainbow Bridge. 'How do you make a universe? All it needs is the energy of a large hydrogen bomb. You confine this in some way to squeeze a small portion of our Universe down into a mini Black Hole. Such a Black Hole does not live very long . . . it will explode within about 10 to the minus thirteen of a second . . . Inside the child universe, completely separate from our space and time, the whole cycle of inflation, steady expansion, formation of galaxies and the evolution of life could have run its course, while we were still wondering if we had made another universe.'[7]

Some scientists, thank whatever gods there may be, can still be poets, and can still make use of the Rainbow Bridge.

We write of millions of light years between transmission and reception of signals from deep space. Yet we are receiving them in the Now. Just as the brushwork and inspiration of a long-dead artist meet the eye and the understanding of the observer in the Now, and inform that Now, so too does the pulse from the distant star meet and inform the Now of the observer on Earth. To an observer, the Big Bang is no further away, and no closer, than an event that took place a second ago (or a 10^{-13} second ago).

The pleasure and thrill of discovery experienced by the astronomer and the futurologist are both experienced in this present moment. In the Tao there is no past nor future, only an eternal now.

The human brain has its two hemispheres: the left to do with analysis and linear thinking, the right to do with feelings, lateral thought and intuition. The best scientists are those that cross the Rainbow Bridge that joins them. Indeed the best scientists would say there is no science without that journey; there may be technology, applied science, but no discovery, no pushing of the frontiers.

For it is on the Rainbow Bridge that the possibility of a balance is found between material fact and mythic significance and the laboratory is transformed into a magician's palace.

Aleister Crowley[8] wrote: 'Magick has led the world from before the beginning of history, if only for the reason that Magick has always been the mother of Science.' Magic is at home in both hemispheres: it observes and analyses, and also allows intuition and ancient folk wisdom due influence. Perhaps magic, together with myth and religion, presents a pathway the West should begin to re-explore in order to regain a *yin/yang* balance, as is already happening in medicine, the subject of my next chapter.

CHAPTER EIGHT

Medicine

The World Health Organization has calculated that four people out of five in the world still rely on traditional medicine.

It is not long – only two or three hundred years – since medicine used myth and magic as much as science: herbs, talismans, and spells as much as the surgeon's knife.

Today's medicine, particularly in the West, is technological, perhaps to an extent that means that a good many babies have been thrown out with the bath water. This is because it confines its view of the body largely to what is observable in material terms.

As few as twenty per cent of doctors' patients anywhere require treatment for acute medical problems: for these, modern technology offers tremendous relief of a kind not previously available. However, 'Most surgeons are using space age technology to patch up our self-abused bodies and to make good the ravages of our modern nutrition and life style.'[1] In fact, most of the other eighty per cent of us can get by very well on non-technological help, often old-fashioned and both preventive and curative.

The *yin/yang* pendulum swings, and many western people have returned to meditation, mind-control, health foods, eastern religions and cosmic consciousness as legitimate means of getting and staying healthy and fit. This is a return to myth and magic perhaps – and why not, if health results? What is encouraging is the fact that on the fringes of western medicine itself there is discernible this wider view, a view which can embrace the best of East and West. In this the body is seen as basically composed of non-material fields of energy.

TAOIST PHYSIOLOGY

The Chinese map of human physiology is similar to the West's in many respects, but it is also markedly different in others.

We see this difference in the Chinese concept of 'organ'. The Western conception of an organ is taken to refer to a physical object found in the body. But traditional Chinese medicine sees the organ as much more than a mere physical object. The nearest approach to the Chinese idea is in Western references to an organ of the brain, by which we mean a region or regions of the brain we fancy to be concerned with some mental or moral quality.

So in China an organ is defined in terms of process – by the way in which bodily (cosmic) energy is stored, transformed and distributed. Such a process may or may not have a physical counterpart. An example of a Chinese organ without a physical counterpart (and therefore disregarded by the West) is what is known as the 'triple burner'. This non-material organ involves, but does not consist of, most of the physical organs of the torso in providing the process necessary to carry out the energy transformations and heat regulation which take place in the body: it performs a 'unitary balancing and controlling' function.

The idea of an organ without a physical reality is no barrier to the work of a Taoist physician. He works as if the human body is at base a complex of fields of energy. The meeting of Taoism with Buddhism was not difficult: the highly cerebral concept contained in the conclusion that 'Form is Void, Voidness is Form' was easily assimilated by the medical practitioner.

Similar to such organs are the acupuncture meridians which may have no physical reality in themselves. The early Chinese, in common with some other people round the world, of whom we have only a few records, saw that internal illness often produced painful areas on the body's external surface which disappeared when a cure was effected. They saw also that sedation or stimulation of various points on the surface of the body affected the functioning of internal organs. After many years of observation of various treatments and their responses, the distribution of such points – four hundred of them in our heads alone – was located and, by joining the points, meridian paths were mapped. These carry the flow of *ch'i* as it circulates round our bodies.

Fundamental to Taoist medicine is the belief that since *ch'i* is a cosmic force, it follows that the meridian pathways connect not only our organs to one another but each of them to the cosmos. The balance of our bodies is therefore a part of the overall balance of the cosmos.

DYNAMIC EQUILIBRIUM

We are not machines, irritating as that fact may be to medical technologists: we are extremely complex creatures, not merely in the physical sense, but in the mental and spiritual senses as well. Western practitioners of alternative medicine talk and practise in terms of each of us being a flux of sophisticated energy, of our consisting of 'base-line primitive activity', and of our being part of etheric force-fields that embrace body, mind and spirit. This is to talk of phenomena which sound very like *ch'i*.

Whatever the basis in reality of these ideas, it is true to say that all living things depend for their survival upon systems of homeostasis. The process of life is not a series of static conditions: it is a constantly changing series of events occurring as fluctuations between complementary processes. According to Taoist medicine, the continued harmony or even existence of the individual, as with the universe itself, depends on the maintenance of this *yin-yang* equilibrium through the five interacting phases of energy transformation at play in nature, and in humans.

HEALTH

Ch'i flows through our meridians constantly, and on the quality of the flow depends the health of our body. When the energy flows through the meridians unimpeded and the various organs are thus in a state of *yin/yang* equilibrium, one is healthy.

Conversely, disease is the manifestation of energy disorder and disequilibrium within our body. If the flow of *ch'i* is too strong or too weak disease will occur.

Some Western treatments depend too much on power: a western alternative medicine regime, megavitamin therapy, for instance, which relies on massive doses of vitamins would seem to be very much too powerful for the good of the patient. So, too, of course, is the general overuse of powerful drugs in allopathic treatment.

Such overuse is encouraged by the way in which Western medical training encourages a doctor to see illness primarily in terms of the observable. He or she diagnoses in terms of the body's plumbing. The doctor's knowledge, of course, cannot be complete. Unlike a household water system we are affected by mind and spirit. The importance of the mind in the health of our bodies is well attested in the work, for instance, of Maltz in his book *Psychocybernetics* and Gawain in her *Creative Visualization*.

The activity of mind in directing our *ch'i* is fundamental in affecting the processes at work in organs and meridians. Misuse will lead to imbalance. Some western alternative treatments seek to correct such a mind/body imbalance: for instance, the Alexander Technique. This is as much concerned with psychosomatic balance as with posture training.

The flow of energy in our body is influenced not only by the conscious and unconscious thoughts we think but by the emotions we experience. If one particular emotion or mode of thinking is habitually emphasized, as in neurosis, a related organ may become over-stimulated, again causing depletion, imbalance and blockage within the meridian system and causing a psychosomatic illness.

Our energy flow may also be influenced towards illness by the fact that too often our mental activity is quite unrelated to our physical activity. Excessive muscular stress in revising for an exam or before making an important presentation are cases in point. It is in their encouragement of 'present-moment thinking' that Taoist disciplines such as *T'ai Chi Ch'uan* are valuable.

DIAGNOSIS

In any case, whatever the cause, disease indicates to Taoist medics that the energy flow needs to be corrected in order that balance may be restored. The earlier diagnosis can take place the better, and often such energy disruption may in fact be detected very early indeed. The physician can do this by taking the pulse. To take the pulse, a Taoist doctor uses three fingers. With these three fingers it is possible to observe six pulses on each wrist, a total of twelve, one for each of the meridians.

By feeling these twelve pulses, the physician can measure the state of *ch'i* in each, and get advance warning of disease from irregularities. Taoist doctors claim also to be able to gain a complete medical history of their patient by the use of the pulses.

For the prevention of diseases, the internal *ch'i* needs to be controlled. After a thorough examination of the patient through the pulse, and by observation and questioning, the physician hopes to follow the precept found in the *Tao Te Ching*, Chapter 54:

> What is motionless is easy to hold;
> What is not yet foreshadowed is easy to form plans for;
> What is fragile is easy to break;
> What is minute is easy to disperse.
> Deal with a thing before it comes into existence.

RESTORING BALANCE

For the prevention or cure of disease through the control of
ch'i, it is again the energy pathways that the doctor uses. He or
she cannot act on them directly. The only points at which it is
possible to control the energy flow effectively and predictably
are at the acupuncture points. The chief traditional means of
influence is by inserting and manipulating a needle, hence the
name. (Interestingly, in a remote part of Brazil, Indians use
blowpipes to shoot tiny arrows into what appear to resemble
acupuncture points.)

Acupuncture points may be mobilized by needle, and also by
pressure and massage, or heat treatment. Whatever method is
used, the aims of the doctor are the same, namely, to restore
the balance of *yin* and *yang* by stimulation or sedation: to
encourage the flow of *ch'i*, or to slow it.

The Chinese were not alone in their discoveries. Even today
in parts of Africa, cures are effected by manipulating parts of
the body; the same sort of thing is done by Eskimos using sharp
stones. One wonders if a similar skill was once more widely
known, and if so, what happened to it.

Acupuncture, the use of the needle, is a cold, *yin*, treatment
and is largely used by physicians for correcting *yang* excesses
and the relief of pain. For the relief of pain, it is claimed that
acupuncture is successful in 93 per cent of cases.[2]

Acupressure, a variety of which the Japanese know as *shiatsu*,
operates on the acupuncture points without the use of needles.
In it the doctor uses the tip or nail of thumb or forefinger, or
the knuckle of the second finger or a blunt needle, rather like
the rubber tip of a pencil.

The doctor may, instead, use heat treatment on the acupuncture points. This *yang* treatment is mainly used to cope with
excesses of cold *yin*. It is done through the burning of the
mugwort plant. Not so long ago, the burning took place directly
on the surface of the skin; nowadays the doctor burns the leaves
in a container which is then held close to the chosen acupuncture
point.

Doctors often use heat treatment in conjunction with acupuncture. In this way they can control the flow of *ch'i* more precisely.

Western medicine recognizes some of the meridians and many of the acupuncture points. Acupuncture points may have been used by people all over the world: it would be strange if the development of human medicine in different parts of the world did not converge. It is true to say, however, that as regards traditional methods, those owed to the Taoists were and remain the most systematized.

HERBALISM

Earliest traditional curative methods included the extensive use of herbs. Today, these are being rigorously investigated to find ways in which they may add to western medical procedures. Their use has a long history in China – and indeed throughout the world. The oriental herb most people have heard of is probably ginseng, which has been reputed to have near miraculous powers. It is a strongly *yang* herb and is used to correct sluggishness caused through an excess of *yin* by burning up wastes and thus encouraging the flow of *ch'i* along the meridians and organs. It has been used by athletes and astronauts to enhance energy resources. In this it is like heat treatment. On the opposite side, chrysanthemum is believed to be a cold, *yin* plant and is customarily used in allaying fevers. Combinations of herbs, some of them toxic, are commonly used: 3000 years of experience has taught Chinese physicians appropriate mixtures, some of which enable the effects of the otherwise toxic herbs to be neutralized.

Chinese pharmacopoeias are said to date back to 3000 BC. The herbs were used then, as now, not so much to attack the diseases frontally, but to restore the body's dynamic balance to normal. A systematic list of medicinal herbs drawn up in the 16th century by a herbalist, Li Chih Shen, is still extensively used in China and its updating is being supported by the World Health Organization, the Ford Foundation and the like.

BREATHING

Not all medicine, either preventive or remedial, needs a doctor. Many people remain in good health when all around are off with the 'flu, and such healing either takes place by itself, or by means of do-it-yourself methods, including breathing exercises and diet.

There are forty distinct methods of breathing recognised by Taoists. Some methods aim at clearing the head, some at renewing sexual potency, and some at healing wounds as well as curing disease. All of them are based on *yin* and *yang*, the rules of cyclic change, and, importantly, on mental application.

Visualization of the passage of the *ch'i* along the meridians and limbs is of importance: such autosuggestion as this is now recognized in the West as being of value in autogenic cures, together with the calming of the body and mind through relaxation exercises, meditation and the like. Such do-it-yourself methods do not necessarily need knowledge of acupuncture points or meridian pathways, though it does increase their effectiveness if these are known, and using the mind to imagine the flow of *ch'i* and to channel the breath most certainly increases their effectiveness.

DIET

One of the biggest changes in our environment over the last hundred years has been in the kinds of food we eat. What may appear to be a balanced diet may in fact be seriously unbalanced due to the often unknown effects of additives. Yet of all human activities, diet is the one which is most likely to affect health.

A non-Taoist regime that is based on the concept of *yin/yang* is one developed by George Ohsawa, a Japanese who cured himself of tuberculosis by means of a regime he came to call Macrobiotics. According to Ohsawa, *yin* and *yang* govern the foods we eat. *Yin* foods include drinks and fruits, food with sweet, sour or hot flavours, and which have an open texture. They are green, blue or purple. *Yang* foods are animal foods, cereals and some vegetables. They are hard and dense and red, orange or yellow. Followers of macrobiotics agree with Taoists in saying that all disease is caused by a *yin/yang* imbalance in the body.

'We in the West eat too much protein, too little cereal fibre, too many refined foods, too much sugar, and too much of everything. Macrobiotics put this right . . .'[3] Macrobiotics is more than just a way of eating, and more than an alternative medicine: it is a way of life that has strong Taoist associations.

A similar Taoist diet supports Ohsawa and adds consideration of cyclic change. For instance, sour foods are recommended for balancing the liver, hot foods for balancing the lungs, and so on. An ideal daily diet contains all five varieties of food: sour, bitter, sweet, hot and salty, with more or less of each according to the needs of each individual. Foods which are prone to cause an imbalance in our system are fat, cold and raw foods, much liquid and very dry or excessively bitter food.[4]

A stricter Taoist diet (*Ch'ang Ming*) is strict indeed. Foods we can never eat include processed grain foods, deep fried food, coffee, alcohol, tobacco, chocolate and other sweets, spices, rock salt, mustard, pepper, vinegar, pickles, curry, red meats, salmon, tuna, mackerel, shark, swordfish or whale, sugar, ice cream, jellies, synthetic fruit juices, potatoes, tomatoes, aubergines, rhubarb, spinach, meat extracts, soups or gravies, cheese, milk, butter, boiled or fried eggs, lard or dripping from animals, and any fat birds or fish.

Strictly following this regime for three years will result, it is said, in the creation of new skin tissue throughout the organs, flesh and muscles. By ten years it is claimed that there will be a renewal of all nails, teeth and bones.[5]

MAGIC

A further Taoist treatment should be mentioned. This is the use of magical talismans. Their use has no doubt become less common, but it may be that their turn will come again, if only because of the increasing knowledge of placebos. Studies have shown that up to 60 per cent of patients get better when given quite useless tablets, although there are some people who believe that the tablets may not be quite neutral, believing that it is possible for a good doctor to impart some kind of healing pattern on the pills. It is interesting that practitioners of radionic therapy believe that such psychic healing energy patterns actually do affect the bodily energy fields.

The treatment of a sick person by talisman is described in full in Legeza's *Tao Magic*. Whether or not it illustrates the placebo effect, it certainly illustrates a deep belief in the power of faith. Briefly, it goes as follows:

The patient tells the Taoist doctor of his or her symptoms, and is led to the image of the Yellow Emperor and bows four times. The doctor recites seven incantations to do with the making of the talisman and also to summon the spirits of the appropriate branch of medicine. Then the doctor paints the charm, silently repeating the Yellow Emperor's chant for healing. When finished, he writes '*chih ling*' (meaning 'induced to come') at the top of the paper. He sprinkles three drops of water on the 'summoning the spirits' charm, takes a mouthful of water and sprays it over the talisman he has just created. Then he makes the healing spirit incantation, clicks his teeth three times to denote a pause, bows, picks up the talisman and retires. Finally, he wraps the talisman in white paper and gives it to the patient with instructions on how to burn it (to send it to the spirits) and what additional drugs to take. The patient must take the talisman home in his or her left hand.[6]

Before scoffing, Westerners should think of their own deep feelings about the doctor and the power apparently residing in the medical books and instruments in the consulting room.

CONCLUSION

The definition of science is, as we have seen, 'knowledge ascertained by observation and experiment, critically tested, systematized and brought under general principles . . .' The Chinese would claim, with justification, that their study of those intangible pathways of *ch'i* as a means of achieving internal and external *yin/yang* harmony satisfies such criteria, sometimes on the operating table, certainly in the doctor's surgery, and in breathing exercises, diet and the like.

It can never be argued that Chinese medicine is superior to that of the West. Both are products of different cultures, those of the West exhibiting many characteristics to be expected of a technological society. It is not so long ago, however, that the West's medicine was as influenced by myth and what appears to be magic as is traditional Eastern medicine. What is sad is that the Chinese to an extent, and the Third World generally, are in the process of adopting the methods of the West, dazzled perhaps by the technology, and may be in danger of losing much that is of value in their own culture.

On the other hand, it is heartening that an increasing number of people in the West, including doctors, are beginning to explore and develop methods that more fully recognize our complex nature and often include a consideration of mental and spiritual factors in the total picture of our health. Into this wider perspective, a recognition of the concepts of energy and balance objectified in the *yin* and the *yang* will certainly play a large and increasingly important part.

It is in the next chapter that I look at the ways in which people may become spiritually and mentally happier and more balanced in themselves and in society.

CHAPTER NINE

Completeness

Taoism has been on the scene for 3000 years, and has gone through many phases of development. It has departed quite markedly from the Way at times, becoming sometimes a political force, sometimes even a revolutionary party. It has sometimes degenerated into what appears to be a primitive form of religion, as well as representing a high philosophy which provides a practical way of living for men and women.

Whatever the manifestation, the one common strand is the belief that the interaction of *yin* and *yang* is the one basic universal law governing change. Even the basest practices keep that belief alive, for even a burglar can aspire to becoming a Superior Burglar, and a martial artist a *Ning-wa* thug, through observing their interplay: what they will not become is a Sage, though eventually even that is not impossible. Observation of the *yin* and the *yang* must eventually lead to wisdom, if the burglar and the thug are given sufficient time.

Essentially, Taoists believe that body, mind, spirit (and cosmos) are not separated. The study of *yin* and *yang* can lead to personal integration, internally within the psychophysical organism, and externally with other persons, all living creatures, and the cosmos.

People, they believe, may master the physical environment through the art or science of *feng shui*, through balancing out the *ch'i* as it runs through the dragon veins. Similarly, they believe that people may maintain health through the practice of acupuncture and other means for balancing out the *yin* and the *yang* as the *ch'i* ebbs and flows within the body.

There are two trinities in Taoism. There is the individual's body/mind/spirit trinity. There are also three aspects of the cosmos: the physical environment, individuals, and their social environment. Beyond, above and permeating both trinities there is the *Tao*, informing the world with *ch'i*, the latter being kept in balance by *yin* and *yang*, and eventually – through *Wu Hsing*, the cycle of the Five Elements – returning to its source.

This chapter firstly examines the popular religion which is said to most resemble Taoism, namely Zen; then the means by which Taoist men and women seek to increase their spiritual stature; and finally the means by which they become more effective as members of society. The second of these is to do with the ways by which Taoists strive to give themselves time to achieve full spiritual development through the pursuit of immortality. The last involves consideration of how they maintain their poise in interpersonal interaction and of how this is done through the practice of self-cultivation in *T'ai-Chi Ch'uan*.

ZEN AND TAOISM

What has Taoism to teach those from the West who seek spiritual development? Taoism in China has often been debased in the temples of the cities and towns and often seems quite at odds with classical Taoism.

Perhaps the question need not be asked, because many would say that Taoism has already entered the West, not only in martial arts and acupuncture but also through Zen Buddhism. There are good reasons for saying so. For instance, there appear to be similarities of practice leading to spontaneity of action, for example, the ideal of Zen and of Taoism. They also share a common history, for Zen is the result of the union of Buddhism and Taoism.

Indian Buddhism entered China around the first century AD. At first it was badly received, perhaps because of the ritual mendicacy of the monks, so much at odds with the Chinese belief in personal endeavour. But by the sixth century many of the Indian schools were well established, and were adding to the existing tensions between Confucianism, with its high-minded codes of behaviour, and the complementary freedom of Taoism.

One can envisage Taoism flowing along its watercourses amongst the rocks of Confucianism and Indian Buddhism. It shared something of value with both. With Confucianism it shared a knowledge of the *Tao*, and the mysterious workings of *yin* and *yang*. With Buddhism it shared the distinction of being a meditative discipline, aware of the primacy of mind.

It therefore had much to teach the Buddhists, who had got bogged down in philosophical and psychological enquiry. For ordinary seekers after enlightenment, Buddhism was doubtless getting too forested to see any trees, or even a way through the forest to the slopes of the mountain. Taoism was mystically respectable, seemed to be not out of touch with reality in the earthy as well as transcendental sense, and therefore was welcomed by Buddhists.

The Ch'an school of Buddhism that emerged brought a new and unique insistence on direct im-mediate realization of Reality, a 'direct existential grasp of reality'.

There is no doubt that the Ch'an Buddhists of the T'ang period (7th–10th Century) were true inheritors of the thought and spirit of Chuang Tsu. The kind of thought and culture represented by him was what transformed speculative Buddhism into the practical Buddhism which flourished in China and, later, Japan.

Zen Buddhism developed in Japan from, and in reaction to, Chinese Ch'an in much the same way as Ch'an developed in reaction to Indian Buddhism. Each race brings its own flavour and approach to Buddhism. Japan brought its own flavour to Ch'an, and changed that rather happy religion into one of harsher discipline of a kind to be expected of the Japanese, with their Samurai tradition. In Zen, as is well known, enlightment (*satori*) is only acquired by undergoing a severe training, 'as ruled and fettered as the result is free'. As such, Zen suited the Japanese perfectly: whether it is translating so well to the West, another century or so (if we are spared) will tell.

Zen has moved on from its roots, so that it is doubtful whether today's Taoism has anything of value to learn from it. Taoism has not moved from its origins.

IMMORTALITY

Taoists are no different from other people in wishing to aspire to the heights of human development, to become what is most succinctly put in the use of the phrase 'one with the gods'. They aim at immortality, no less. This is not the same as 'life eternal', nor is it an aspect of the concept of reincarnation.

Unlike the followers of most religions, the pragmatic Chinese could see no certainty of a life hereafter. It is true that they prudently prepared for the possibility of post-death existence in some form by ensuring propitious burials for their ancestors, themselves, and their family; but what life in the spirit world involved was a closed book to them. They came to know enough of Indian, including Buddhist, thought to be aware of the possibility, given time, of attaining the highest development. But time was the one commodity, in the absence of a belief in reincarnation, that they did not have. It seemed prudent therefore to put off the moment of death for as long as possible – indeed, for ever, if that was possible. They aimed at immortality, or more accurately, they aimed to join the Immortals, those nine very human Taoist figures that live for ever in the clouds, occasionally descending to earth amongst us.[1] To become a Sage is a step towards becoming an immortal, the highest state to which men and women may aspire.

So developed the Chinese interest in alchemy, including a form that is uniquely Chinese.

Alchemy itself is not unique to the Chinese: it has been a world-wide practice, a search for a pill or substance that would confer the benefit of immortality or at least great longevity upon its creator.

The creation of the Golden Pill involved the coupling of *yang* chemicals with *yin*. One of the elements associated with the male was sulphur. One of the elements associated with the female was mercury. By mixing in designated and secret quantities, and heating and cooling the mixtures for designated and secret periods of time, the Golden Pill which conferred immortality was made.

As a result of swallowing the elixir, the mind was ready to dissolve into the pure spirit of the Void. One had then acquired a body beyond a body; one was able to leave the body at will and 'soar among the stars'. This soaring was a state of consciousness in which all sense of self and other, of heaven and earth had vanished: nothing remained but pure Void, a limitless ocean of *chi'i*. This super-consciousness, this Self-realization was the aim of most alchemists throughout the world: to achieve some sort of mystical end to duality, to absorption in the Absolute, a return to what the Chinese called the *Tao*.

Where the Chinese appear to have been unique is in the development of a method peculiarly their own, a logical interpretation of *yin/yang* theory.

One of the classics dealing with alchemy is called *The Ts'an T'ung Chi'*. This appears to be a straightforward account of methods to transmute base metals into gold, but it can also be interpreted as ways in which experimenters could create the elixir of life. It can also, and this is what is unique to the Chinese, be interpreted as explaining a method of converting one's body through sexual practices into that spirit-body that will live for ever. It is truly a remarkable book.

This other method involved the *yin* and *yang* aspects of the human body and utilized the bodily sexual fluids of the alchemists. '. . . We see that the ancients really attained long life by the help of the seed-energy present in their own bodies (and not by swallowing elixirs . . .)'[2] 'Each time that Heaven unites itself with the Earth seize for yourself the secret springs of the creative activities of yin and yang.'[3]

By the exercise of extreme self control, which in men involved prevention of ejaculation, and by utilizing secret practices, the sexual fluids, known as *ching*, were converted first to *ch'i* and then into pure spirit, known as *shen*.

Successful practice of the path of union of the sexes also involved attention to the breath, to quietude of mind, and the repression of passion. Successfully achieved, the bones were said to become indestructible, tough and resilient, as supple as an infant's. This seemed like rejuvenation.

The practices of Indian Tantra are similar in some respects to what is described here: as we saw earlier, Tantra is an effort to redress the balance between the male and female aspects of the deity. As such, it may be that Chinese practices fed back to India at the time of cross-fertilization I described in the opening section of this chapter.

Be that as it may, there are many stories in China of hundred year old men having upright bearings, unlined faces and black hair on their heads, clearly as fit and supple as men a fraction of their age.

It is worth remarking, too, that we saw that the *Cheng Ming* diet claims to enable people to achieve the same rejuvenation of the bones and organs of the body.

However, it must be said that alchemical practices of any sort are not to be found discussed at any length in the classical Taoism of Chuang Tzu and Lao Tsu. The former in particular is dismissive of them, hinting that the goal is a limited one and not commensurate with the effort involved. He observed that it missed the real point, which was that the Sage 'delights in early death, he delights in old age' and the 'True Man of Old knew nothing of loving life and hating death.' He went on to say that anyone who clearly understands the *Tao* does not rejoice at life or repine at death, for he knows that these are not final' – a reference here, perhaps, to reincarnation.

This way of life – the *Tao* – advocated by Chuang Tzu was the one common to mystics and religious the world over: a quieting of the spirit, a concentration on meditation in a quiet place, and a seeking to experience the eternal in the present moment.

Before moving on from this section, it is worth saying that this interest in sex and old age and death may have something to say of value to our age, with its present preoccupation with those very areas of life. It is possible that Taoist practices could bring back dignity where it has been lost.

LIVING IN SOCIETY

Human beings who seek enlightenment may often cut themselves off from their fellow men and women. Taoists do not. Other people are important to our full development. So they are concerned to perfect relationships, since they will know that everyone is part of a universal network. Since minds are not separate from bodies, such gentle meditative arts as *T'ai-Chi Ch'uan* may be practised. In these slow and graceful physical exercises, most often done in the early morning with the dew still wet on the grass, the aim is to guide the internal *ch'i* in a way which exactly mirrors cosmic law, and to aim at dynamic balance in the body and an interaction with other bodies in the same way.

In achieving such a dynamic balance in *T'ai-Chi Ch'uan*, there are two important rules.

The first is to do with energy-conservation, and is based on a belief that change is cyclic. Lao Tzu has much to say in general on the subject. For example, when he says that since everything under the sun is subject to birth, growth, maturity, decline and death, it follows that an individual must make sure 'not to live too quickly', to have always something in reserve, for decline always follows fullness. In moving, one should never extend one's body completely. To do so, leaves nothing in reserve: in martial arts it will be easy for one's partner to pull you over. Similarly it is wise never to use all of one's energy: just so much, and no more. Go only to a certain point, then draw inward again to the centre in order to gather again your energy. This law of reversion depends on a practical realization of *yin* and *yang* and the theory of Cyclic Change. In relating to others, Sages are careful not to over-commit themselves, but to relate cautiously, respectfully, giving way, saving their own face and that of others.

The second rule is to do with the mere act of standing. This, again firmly based on the *yin* and *yang*, advocates that one should never stand with one's weight evenly balanced: instead, the practitioner is enjoined to stand 'like an unbalanced scale'. Only so can one be ready to move, not be caught flat-footed, or 'double-heavy' as the Chinese call it. To stand evenly flat-footed is to be sluggish, and incapable of quick response.

As in *T'ai-Chi Ch'uan*, so in life generally: it does not do to rest on one's laurels, better far to preserve a readiness of body, mind and spirit for further action. Such maintenance of balance enables the bodymind to move the *ch'i* easily, naturally, smoothly and continuously in full accord with circumstances, whatever they might be, and particularly in communion and communication with one's fellows.

There is in *T'ai-Chi Ch'uan* a training exercise called 'sticking hands' in which by touching hands, partners can learn to interpret the state of readiness of the other's mind and body. The way in which a hand retreats can signal a shift of body weight or change in posture. In such ways a student learns to anticipate an attack: it is as though you learn to listen to the other's non-verbal messages through your hands. There is an increased awareness of the body language of other people to be gained by such alert attention to the game. At advanced levels, it gives practice in awareness of the currents of the environment, so that a martial artist or a Sage is never 'caught napping'. Such a one is always aware, always ready to deal appropriately with any of life's little surprises – or big ones. In an earthquake, such a one would initially sit still with every sense alert for the current of events, in order to avoid death most expeditiously, or to meet it without flinching. It is in such mindful coolness that the connection that runs from Taoism through Ch'an Buddhism to Zen Buddhism is most clearly seen.

There is no room in the proper practice of *T'ai-Chi Ch'uan* or martial arts – or everyday living – for personal animosity: all the attention is on such listening, such a gathering of energy, such a care for the maintenance of balance. An expert martial artist reacts to the total situation: 'For example, I would start to move and my opponent would throw a kick and I would realize that I was moving out of the way of a kick. But I was doing it before I knew why! I just moved, and they would throw a kick and miss!'[3] This reminds me of the story told by Chuang Tzu of the old man who fell into a cataract and came out downstream quite unharmed. Asked to comment, he said '. . . Plunging in with the whirl, I came out with the swirl . . . I accommodate myself to the water, not the water to me. And so I am able to deal with it . . .'

Taoists seek to control their *ch'i*. By training their minds and their breaths (coarse *ch'i*), they are enabled to respond to outward circumstances naturally and entirely appropriately. Martial arts masters continually enquire of their students whether the concentration of *ch'i* has enabled the student to 'return to the pliability of the infant'. This is a reference to a return to the state of the 'uncarved block', a state without preconceptions or plans, entirely focused on, and entirely at one with, the total situation. *T'ai Chi Ch'uan* aims to bring the physical, emotional, mental and spiritual energies into dynamic balance once again, not by any superhuman effort of will, but spontaneously and naturally, in the way that water finds appropriate means to flow downhill.

CONCLUSION

Taoist practices are designed to lead to appropriateness of behaviour in private and social environments.

Believing that they are physically, mentally and spiritually integral to the universe, Taoist Sages are practitioners of meditation in action: their early morning *T'ai Chi Ch'uan* exercises illustrate this. They gently exercise their bodies and minds in order to operate harmoniously with the laws of nature, of which the goings-on of others are a part. Believing as they do that everyone's daily activities evoke a response from the totality of the universe, they seek to operate harmoniously with circumstances, as a stream of water negotiates its way to the ocean.

Whatever special practices the Sage may indulge in, he or she is mindful at all times, and will be careful to try to conform throughout the day to eight simple principles, so present-day Masters such as Ni, Hua Ching, tell us. These are: early rising and early retiring, practising serenity in sitting and moving, heeding one's words, avoiding excessive sexual activity and excessive indulgence in foods, and being generally abstinent in one's involvement in unnecessary activities. In all, there is a concentration on quietude.

> There is a thing inherent and natural,
> Which existed before heaven and earth.
> Motionless and fathomless,
> It stands alone and never changes;
> It pervades everywhere and never becomes exhausted.
> It may be regarded as the Mother of the universe.
> I do not know its name.
> If I am forced to give it a name,
> I call it *Tao* and I name it as supreme.
>
> (CHAPTER 25)

Human beings, Lao Tsu and Chuang Tsu would say, are not meant officiously to strive, but are meant to pursue the way of purposeful non-action, *wu wei*, following the manifestations in *yin* and *yang* of the *Tao*.

They do this in the certain knowledge that there is nothing else that can be done. This is certainly not to the taste of the Western world. However, it may be the only way that will save humankind from its own extinction, and this theme is pursued in my final chapter.

CHAPTER TEN

The Tao of Power

This book has been about change and balance; about the belief of Taoists in the union of the Azure Dragon and the White Tiger from which issues the sustaining creative principle, the breath of *ch'i*. The book has also been about an interloper disturbing the process. That interloper is the human race, the individuals of which have discovered in their expanding brain and their inventive fingers a power which appeared to give them control of their destiny on this planet – for of all the creatures on earth, only we humans have effective power to control change. We thought we had got rather good at this. But our chickens are coming home to roost in a mucky farmyard of weapons, pollution, loss of flora and fauna, climatic changes, uglification of cities and landscapes, famines, non-accountable multinational companies, and so on and so on and so on.

POWER

Taoism remains one human response to that loss of direction. It too is about power, and it is worth reminding ourselves that the title of its basic collection of writings, the *Tao Te Ching*, translates as 'The Way and its Power', and it gives practical hints as to the ways in which human beings may bring themselves into harmony with cosmic power. Cosmic power is everywhere apparent from the roar of an earthquake to the falling of an acorn, from the formation of a Black Hole to the life of a sub-atomic particle.

Human beings, themselves part of nature, are subject to and have access to this power. For most of history they have been aware of their connectedness with the natural world and have not departed far from the ways of nature. Thus natural processes have enabled them to move forward with *yang* strength, and to withdraw with *yin* where necessary. But in our own present age they have become enamoured of the power of the Azure Dragon, to the detriment of themselves and their surroundings. Conversely, they too often take on yin characteristics when to do so is not appropriate or fruitful, for instance in acquiescing in the rape of the earth by political masters. In short, they have lost their connectedness with their roots, and the knowledge that their plans are best brought to fruition by thoughtful and harmonious integration with the processes of nature. As a modern master writes: 'Harmony is the subtle yet inviolable power of the universe, whereas force and violence are aberrations. This is fundamental universal law. Every positive manifestation in the universe comes forth as the result of the creative, harmonized union of yin and yang energies ... Following the inherent order of the universe results in harmony and balance; opposing the cosmic principle of natural order creates destruction.'[1]

THE POWER OF TAO

Such reminders as are contained in the *Tao Te Ching* are not, at first reading, earth-shattering. They stress the need for harmony and balance to an extent that makes them appear otherworldly, if they can be understood at all. But they *are* about this world and its human inhabitants.

The previous chapter ended on a note that evoked a picture of ancient Taoists, busy cultivating their own little plot, and living out their lives in innocent pleasures. But it should be remembered that such people affected their times, and continue to do so.

Taoists are people. All people seek to find a way of life that leads to happiness. Some are forced to find this happiness in sheer survival, some find it in ephemeral pleasures, and others find it in what appear to them to be eternal truths. Taoists are among the latter, and perhaps it is because they are more skilful than most that in this present day and age it must appear that they are non-activists in the grand struggles of humankind. Taoism is about eternal truth and therefore its followers are even now affecting our times. But they are not obtrusive, and err on the side of caution; for, as I wrote earlier, life provides choices that, once made, may not only turn out to be in error, but are also irrevocable.

COLLECTIVISM VERSUS INDIVIDUALISM

The trouble with writing about modern problems for a western readership is that one is expected to come up with the kind of instant answer which, it is thought, if put across sufficiently persuasively will save the world and its inhabitants from the results of their foolishness. To join a political party, a church, a union, a religious sect or whatever seems to many to provide a possibility of righting wrongs and regaining balance. This leads, as it always has, to fragmentation and disharmony. As Ben Willis writes: 'Consider the facts. The very fabric of our social order is implicit with the enforcing of boundaries – of kin, class, territory and ownership, implicit with building walls between other people and ourselves. We are part of a clan, family, team, profession, business or nation . . . We don't harmonize or co-operate – we isolate and oppose. We don't unify – we make distinctions.'[2]

Taoism, in contrast, is about individuals: about each man's and woman's individual response to his or her individual universe. It is not, and never has been, a movement – it is not within its nature to be so. We wrote in Chapter Three that both Lao Tsu and Chuang Tsu were not in favour of collectivism, and energetically avoided participation in affairs of state. The most that a modern Taoist will say is: 'The Taoist teachings are mostly concerned with the development of the individual human being. With regard to the whole human society, the principle of "non-action" (*wu wei*) may be considered a guideline for a future of peace and safety.'[3]

Herein lies the difficulty in addressing modern men and women, who are increasingly collectivized and socialized into judging themselves in terms of material possessions, affiliations, and the opinions of others, and who are increasingly persuaded that to every problem there is somebody else or a group of people with an instant solution. In fact there are no such fast remedies for most of our problems – only, perhaps, swift retribution. Ni, Hua Ching is here telling us to give *yin* and *yang* room for manoeuvre.

AN EXAMPLE OF *YIN* BALANCE

Perhaps the most obvious (but not necessarily the best) example of *yin* reasserting itself today is the topic we looked at in Chapter Two. In this we saw how the world of religion had down-graded the feminine aspect of God, the female principle in the world, the *yin* principle of the cosmos, and how there is occurring a change back to older and wiser ways. The Gaia hypothesis carries echoes of the Great Earth Mother, and the Green Movement, at its best, seeks only to serve Her. We have Mary and Tara and a growing tendency towards the full recognition once more of the need for a female priesthood – a tendency that is at its most effective when individual women get on with the job and do not wait for synods.

Feminism at its best is about reinstating this feminine creative principle, which is the opposite of the masculine in every possible way. At its worst, and this is true of most present-day attempts to redress balance, many such feminist efforts at reinstatement take on the characteristics of the *yang* domination they seek to redress. This is hardly surprising, but Taoists would say that it must be counterproductive. Nevertheless, I believe that it is in the feminist movement that the White Tiger has most chance of present-day recognition. Women, at any rate in *yang*-dominated times, are not thrusting and outward-looking:

they are small group (family) oriented, conservers and nourishers. A full recognition of this will immediately align them with that necessary ingredient of balance, the *yin* White Tiger. It most certainly does not mean that they stay in the kitchen and bed for the pleasure of their Azure Dragons. Instead, it may mean that they will be welcomed in taking their full place once more in increasingly balanced affairs of the spirit and the world.

TAOISM TODAY

There is little doubt, in the meantime, that we live in a world that is increasingly unbalanced, a world in which the Dragon and the Tiger are finding it increasingly difficult to achieve their fruitful mating. Yet, to an extent, it has always been so. One has only to dip into the *Tao Te Ching* to see that the sort of problems we face today have been those faced by people throughout the ages. There are constant references to armies, politicians, the effects of war, taxation, rebellion, quarrelling, and so on – all the ills to which men and women are, and will continue to be, prey.

Now, as throughout history, the majority of human beings are engaged in the sheer business of survival. Others, as throughout history, once their primary needs are satisfied, have spent their time in finding a sort of happiness in activities that have exploited their planet and their fellows. It is a sad fact that in one way or another most men and many women have ignored the ways of life of the religious and mystics, all of which aim to align themselves with cosmic power.

Yet we have seen throughout the book that balance is essential to the physical and developmental health of us all. Constant reference has been made to the fact that nature – the Tao – call it what you will, tends to dynamic balance, to homeostasis. Without this underlying tendency to balance, the human race might well have perished long ago.

Perhaps this is why Taoists, accepting this, are seen as taking what appears to be a very laissez-faire attitude to life and its vicissitudes. It is the behaviour resulting from this cosmic trust that may give modern Westerners a mistaken idea that Taoism is of little practical use in facing the modern world and its problems.

Against this are three facts. One is that the *yin/yang* balance is a dynamic balance, and not a state of rest or cessation of activity. Another fact is that the *yin/yang* balance is not dependent on human endeavour. The reverse is true: a fully developed person realizes a dependence on *yin/yang* and acts with an energy that is unencumbered with human preconceptions or societal pressures, and which will tend towards harmony. The third observed fact is one I hope to have illustrated; that almost all Taoist-based activities are in fact intensely practical and active. For example, *feng shui hsien sheng* (masters) seek gently to observe and use dynamic balance in agriculture, town planning and interior decoration. They do this in order that human beings may develop a similar balance and maintain a connection with cosmic power.

What is different, and what causes difficulty to many westerners, is the stepping back as it were of the Taoist from heavy handed manipulation of the environment and his or her fellows, and the advance towards an intelligent participation in that environment and the affairs of those neighbours in ways which seek to take the larger view, to anticipate the cooperation of nature and the environment rather than its conquest. Of course at a superficial level there does appear to be a contradiction in all this. How can one talk of the absence of manipulation in the same breath as talking of active participation in environmental trends?

In modern parlance, the practitioner of Taoism aims to be like a glider pilot, pressing on towards a safe landing by making use of the air currents to arrive at the goal. While he may appear to be alone in his glider, he has the company of mighty forces. In writing about Thor Heyerdahl's amazing voyage across the Pacific on a balsa raft, Watts writes that 'Heyerdahl's genius was that he had a basic trust in the unified system of his own organism and the ecosystem of the Pacific . . . By virtue of this attitude he was helped along by events he had not consciously expected.'[6] This is always true of reliance on the method of *wu wei*.

The Azure Dragon and White Tiger are always present, and in the worst and best of circumstances there is always to be found the seed-pearl of its opposite. It is up to the wise man and woman to seek it out and nurture it. The heavenly pair will aid.

GETTING IN ON THE BALANCING ACT

How may a son or daughter of the twentieth century encourage the mating? Perhaps merely (!) by snatching a couple of periods of twenty minutes every day in order to sit. That's all – to sit, aware of breathing and passing thoughts, turning one's back on mundane affairs, no matter how pressing. That's all that Chuang Tsu would have wanted, as a start. And it is practical advice, even at an everyday level, for it mobilizes little used aspects of the human brain. 'We are at present using but a small part of the human brain. The Taoists have shown us the Way towards using all of it, the Way towards mastery of the physical dimension of existence through spiritual mastery and the use of the inner creative power and internal energy we all have. It was always a Way which is in our hands and depends on our will, and it was made for natural life in *this* world . . .'[4] It is quiet contemplation, easy meditation, leading the individual forward with the stream.

A thread that runs through all areas of Taoist thought and practice is that of *connectedness:* individual human to all other humans, animals, nature, Gaia, the cosmos itself. At home, to encourage connectedness, the Taoist will surround him- or herself with symbols of *yin* and *yang*; in the garden will be miniature representations of balanced nature. As we saw (p 70) fundamental to Taoist belief is what a modern master has called the 'Universal Energy Net', a unified system of our own organisms and the ecosystem of our environment, of which our thoughts and actions are parts and which directly and unfailingly affect all other of its parts. Such a concept receives, as I showed in Chapter Seven, support and validation from various sectors of Western science, as well as other Eastern religions and Western mystics and poets.

It's a well-known Chinese proverb that says that a journey of a thousand miles must begin with a single step. To snatch those precious forty minutes may in this day and age be the most difficult achievement of all.

Nevertheless, the fact is that once one has taken the first leap of faith that trust in this entails, and has begun to make the practice a regular occasion, one is in the stream, and manipulation and *wu wei* become increasingly indistinguishable. Beginning Taoists find that they start to accept the workings of the Azure Dragon and the White Tiger in their lives, and learn a little more about acceptance of all that life can bring, and please themselves more. In trying to let each day produce for them what it will, they find increased happiness and practical effectiveness. This may sound like a kind of self-justifying teeth-gritting stoicism, but they do not find it so. In fact they find themselves moving towards the lyrical quality of the life of fully committed Taoists, both of the past and of the modern age. This quality is apparent in much of Chuang Tsu's writings, in John Blofeld's descriptions of the hermits he visited in China[5], in some of Alan Watts' writings, and, I believe, is available to anyone; for it is a way of life that is in tune with external nature and inner needs. Nor are Taoists in any sense 'holier than thou'. Their happiness and effectiveness result not in any such attitude, but in an unforced, almost childlike contentment, happiness and fellow-feeling, that emerges in the peculiarly Chinese concept of face.

But such a way of life as these illustrate is not one that leads necessarily to collective action. However, by 'looking out for number one' in this way, action in society and community may follow: individuals may find that they can drift with their personal *wu wei* and find that this is in fact to join a larger stream.

Balance in ecological concerns, for instance, is provided by the individuals who find their stream flowing towards the green movement.

Balance in international power is provided by individuals who flow together in peace groups.

Balance in human need is provided by the people who throw their bread into their stream.

Balance in materialistically-oriented schooling is balanced by the leavening of small alternative schools, started by small numbers of concerned individuals dedicated to encouraging the ideals that naturally arise within men and women, boys and girls, and which are stifled in conventional schools.

And so the list grows.

And so the movements grow, and in this growth they may lose *yin* effectiveness as they move towards adopting dominant and dominating *yang* procedures.

TAOIST ORGANIZATION

This is almost a contradiction in terms, for a developed Taoist aims to keep organization to the minimum, in order to allow the everyday flow of energy to move freely, unconstricted by rules and procedures.

Consequently, a Taoist will believe that the only really effective groupings are those that are small, and which are ready and able to dissolve when their work is done. This is to cook little fish lightly. Apart from the fact that such size and fluidity means they are hard to pin down by opponents, there is the danger that beyond a certain size they become politicized, with AGMs and organizations that ape the political groupings that cause the problems in the first place. Thus the optimum size of a group is that in which everyone is known by each member, as in the hermitages described by Blofeld. As Lao Tsu tells us, people find peace and contentment and effectiveness on a human scale when

they live within sight of their neighbours, And

123

crowing cocks and barking dogs are heard across the
way, Yet they leave each other in peace . . .

This is not to say that there cannot be a loose and fluid feder-
ation of like-minded groups for the exchange of information
and so on, but the emphasis is on being small, loose, local, and
fluid – water has always been a potent symbol of the workings
of the Tao.

Such individuals and small groups, though they may appear
to be fragile and ineffective, sometimes appearing to represent
very forlorn attempts to bring about change, nevertheless
develop and flow like water into the consciousnesses of other
men and women, and provide a leavening that can cause a sea-
change, even a paradigm shift. Think, if you are a Christian, of
the single mustard seed. Think, if you are a Buddhist, of the
Bodhisattva ideal. Think of these as the seeds of change in the
yin/yang symbol.

HOPE

'Power' is a word which today has positive *yang* overtones,
expressive of the domination of rulers. Yet we have all heard
the expression 'the power behind the throne', expressive of a
gentler balancing female counterpoise.

How is the power of *Tao* best to be described? Let us take
water, so often said to be expressive of the *Tao*. Little could be
more fluid and less forceful in its basic form. It can cool the
brow and yet can wear away rock – both in the course of
achieving a needed balance. Air, too, exhibits qualities of both
the White Tiger and the Azure Dragon, cooling the brow and
yet, unheralded, uprooting forests overnight.

Cosmic balance will be achieved.

In an age when *yang* dominates, *yin* is also present behind
the thrones and principalities, to be detected in all aspects that
are not *yang*. By her presence she will bring about a new bal-

ance: while it may take aeons to wear away a rock, a hurricane can arrive overnight.

Finally, what must be emphatically stated once more is that Taoism is not a world-wide church. It is not a movement. Instead it may today provide at least an approach to a perfection of *yin* in a *yang*-dominated world, for it is in all respects a system of belief and living that embodies the opposite of all that is most admired in our hustling mis-directed world.

It is hidden, not obtrusive; personal, not collective.

It is the seed pearl of change.

References

Chapter One: The Concept of Face

(1) Blofeld, John, *I Ching, the Chinese Book of Change*, George Allen & Unwin, 1968.

Chapter Two: Azure Dragon Rampant

(1) Wilson, Martin, *In Praise of Tara*, Wisdom Publications, 1986, Introduction.
(2) Allegro, John, *Lost Gods*, Sphere Abacus, 1977, p 185f.

Chapter Three: The Sage

(1) Maslow, Abraham, *The Farther Reaches of Human Nature*, Viking Penguin Inc, 1971, p 7.
(2) Smith, Elizabeth, *Choose Happiness*, Gateway Books, 1984, pp 57–8.
(3) Merton, Thomas, *The Way of Chuang Tzu*, George Allen & Unwin, 1970, p 141.
(4) Freire, Paulo, *Pedagogy of the Oppressed*, Sheed & Ward, 1972, p 45.

Chapter Four: Cherishing the Water Dragons

(1) Lovelock, James, 'I Speak for the Earth', in *Resurgence* Number 128.
(2) Giles, Herbert A, *Chuang Tzu*, 1889.
(3) Skinner, Stephen, *The Living Earth Manual of Feng Shui*, Routledge 1979.

Chapter Five: Cooking Little Fishes

(1) Goldman, Emma, *The Place of the Individual in Society*, Friends of Malatesta, Buffalo, NY, n.d., p 7.
(2) Godwin, William, *Enquiry Concerning Political Justice*, 1793, chapter on Law.
(3) Devillers, Phillipe, *What They Really Said: Mao*, Macdonald & Co, 1969, p 89.
(4) Woodworth, Fred, *Anarchism*, The Match!, Tucson, Arizona, 1973, p 14.
(5) Erlich, Howard J, *Anarchism and Formal Organisations*, Vacant Lots Press, Baltimore, 1977, pp 5–6.
(6) Phillipe Devillers, *op cit*, p 142.

Chapter Six: The Rainbow Bridge

(1) Watts, Alan, *Tao, the Watercourse Way*, Jonathan Cape, 1976, p 29.
(2) Chang Chung-yuan, *Creativity and Taoism*, Gower Publishing, 1975, p 212.
(3) Alan Watts *op cit*, p 15.

Chapter Seven: Black Holes and Magic

(1) Einstein, Albert, *Out of my Later Years*, Greenwood, 1970.
(2) Emerson, Ralph Waldo, *The Conduct of Life*, Macmillan, 1884.
(3) Kronenberger, Louis, *Company Manners*, Bobbs-Merrill, 1962.
(4) Merrington, Tom, letter to the *Guardian*, 12 January 1988.
(5) Capra, Fritjof, *The Tao of Physics*, Wildwood House, 1975.
(6) Nagel, Thomas, 'What is it Like to be a Bat?' in Hofstadter & Dennet, *The Mind's I*, Harvester Press 1981, p 403n.
(7) Gribbin, John, 'An anniversary of Some Gravity', article in *New Scientist*, 12 November 1987.
(8) Crowley, Aleister, *Magick Without Tears*, Falcon, 1973.

Chapter Eight: Medicine

(1) Stanway, Andrew, *Alternative Medicine*, Macdonald & Janes, 1980, introduction.
(2) Chee Soo, *The Taoist Ways of Healing*, Aquarian Press, 1980, p 111.
(3) Andrew Stanway, *op cit*.

REFERENCES

(4) Ni, Hua Ching, *Tao, the Subtle Universal Law*, Union of Tao and Man, Los Angeles, 1979, Chapter 4.
(5) Chee Soo, *op cit*, Chapter 5.
(6) Legeza, Laszlo, *Tao Magic*, Thames & Hudson, 1975, pp 26–7.

Chapter Nine: Completeness

(1) Blofeld, John, *Taoism: the Quest for Immortality*, George Allen & Unwin, 1979, *passim*.
(2) Wilhelm, Richard, *The Secret of the Golden Flower*, Routledge and Kegan Paul, 1975, p 34.
(3) Chang Chung-yuan, *op cit*, p 134.
(4) Ralston, Peter, 'Consciousness and the Martial Arts', in *Human Potential Resources*, 1982.

Chapter Ten: The Tao of Power

(1) Ni, Hua Ching, *op cit*, p 41.
(2) Willis, Ben, *The Tao of Art*, Century Paperbacks, 1987, p 162.
(3) Ni, Hua Ching, *op cit*, p 140.
(4) Alan Watts, *op cit*, p 122.
(5) Ben Willis, *op cit*, p 167.
(6) John Blofeld, *Taoism, The Quest For Immortality*, Chapter 10.

Bibliography

Allegro, John, *Lost Gods*, Michael Joseph, 1977

Blofeld, John, *I Ching, the Chinese Book of Change*, George Allen & Unwin, 1968

Taoism: the Quest for Immortality, George Allen & Unwin, 1979

Capra, Fritjof, *The Tao of Physics*, Wildwood House, 1975

Chang Chung-yan, *Creativity and Taoism*, Wildwood House, 1975

Chee Soo, *The Taoist Ways of Healing*, Aquarian Press, 1986

Ch'u Ta-Kao, *Tao Tê Ching*, George Allen & Unwin, 1937

Devillers, Phillipe, *What They Really Said: Mao*, Macdonald & Co, 1969

Eitel, E J, *Feng Shui*, 1873

Erlich, Howard J, *Anarchism and Formal Organisations*, Vacant Lots Press, Baltimore, 1977

Freire, Paulo, *Pedagogy of the Oppressed*, Sheed & Ward, 1972

Gawain, Shakti, *Creative Visualization*, Whatever Publishing, California, 1978

Giles, Herbert A, *Chuang Tzu*, 1889

Godwin, William, *Enquiry Concerning Political Justice*, 1793

Goldman, Emma, *The Place of the Individual in Society*, Friends of Malatesta, Buffalo, NY, n.d.

Hofstadter and Dennet *The Mind's I*, Harvester Press, 1981

Jung, C. G. *Psychology and the East*, Princeton University Press, 1978

Lau, D. C, *Tao Te Ching*, Penguin Books, 1963

Legeza, Laszlo, *Tao Magic*, Thames & Hudson, 1975

Lovelock, James, *Gaia: a New Look at Life on Earth*, Oxford University Press, 1982

Maltz, Maxwell, *Psycho-cybernetics*, Prentice Hall, 1960

Maslow, Abraham, *The Farther Reaches of Human Nature*, Viking Press, 1971

Merton, Thomas, *The Way of Chuang Tzu*, George Allen and Unwin, 1970

Ni, Hua Ching, *Tao, the Subtle Universal Law*, Union of Tao and Man, Los Angeles, 1979

BIBLIOGRAPHY

Piaget, J, *The Origins of Intelligence in Children*, Int. University Press, NY, 1952

Ralston, Peter, 'Consciousness and the Martial Arts' in *Human Potential Resources*, 1982

Skinner, Stephen, *The Living Manual of Feng Shui*, Routledge and Kegan Paul 1979

Smith, Elizabeth, *Choose Happiness*, Gateway Books, 1984

Stanway, Andrew, *Alternative Medicine*, Macdonald & Jane, 1980

Toulson, Shirley, *The Celtic Adventure*, Century Hutchinson 1987

Watts, Alan, *Tao, the Watercourse Way*, Jonathan Cape, 1976

Wilhelm, Richard, *The Secret of the Golden Flower*, Routledge and Kegan Paul, 1975

Wilson, Martin, *In Praise of Tara*, Wisdom Publications, 1986

Woodworth, Fred, *Anarchism*, The Match!, Tucson, Arizona, 1973

More paperbacks from

Green Print

The books described on the following pages can be ordered from all competent booksellers. Many book-shops have them in stock. For our current catalogue and to join our free mailing list, write to Green Print, The Merlin Press, 10 Malden Road, London NW5 3HR.

Teaching Green

A parent's guide to education for life on Earth

Damian Randle

The world is going green. But is education keeping up? Parents and teachers must work together to make sure it does. Teaching Green points the way.

Green education will help children to grow as fulfilled, independent and caring people – active democrats co-operating with each other and with the earth. Simple in style, radical in content and outspoken in tone, this book guides parents, teachers and students towards an education that is good for people and good for the earth.

It emphasises emotional, spiritual and physical, as well as intellectual, needs. It stresses the need for children and young people to learn to work together, not against one another. And it uncovers ways of developing technologies, lifestyles and political practices which will enable us to sustain life on earth beyond the current phase of rapacious, anti-ecological industrialism.

Damian Randle shares with the reader the many insights gained by people who are already pioneering new ideas and new techniques. The book is packed with examples of new education in action, and is an inspiration to the rapidly growing number of parents and teachers dissatisfied with education as presently understood.

The author was a teacher for twelve years before becoming joint education officer at the Centre for Alternative Technology, Machynlleth. His last post was as head of faculty at a Community High School near Wolverhampton. He is editor of Green Teacher, an international journal for teachers and educators which he founded in 1986.

The Stolen Future

How to rescue the Earth for our Children

Patrick Rivers

The environment crisis now making headlines is no surprise. Entirely predictable, ignored despite warnings from countless eminent authorities, it has been brewing for aeons: only the timing lay in doubt. For as human beings we suffer from crucial defects built into our nature, and a resultant collective lunacy is now climaxing. By stealing from our children the very future they expect and deserve, we risk becoming just one more endangered species.

The measures that politicians are now hastily assembling amount to little more than delaying tactics. Remedies have to reach root causes. As individuals and as a species we must first acknowledge our unflattering limitations and identify our buried qualities. And then make a pact with the planet on which we totally depend. In short, unless we put Earth first we cannot last.

These are some of the many contentious findings in this well-timed book. Patrick Rivers asks 'If we ignore such a challenge, how can we look our children in the eyes and declare we love them above all else?'.

Tracing the course of human history, he depicts how we have let a male-dominated, over-industrialised society, and the values that go with it, warp our true nature so severely that we have become a species under pandemic stress. Like laboratory rats or caged animals, our behaviour has become freakish and obsessive. As our power has outstripped our sense of responsibility, we have so lost sight of vital connections that we have let world crisis engulf us.

To escape extinction we need to re-create societies where we can regain touch with our roots. Only then can we replace our media-reinforced self-image of a competitive, ruthless and selfish species with one of co-operation, trust, compassion and selfish species with one of co-operation, trust, compassion and tolerance. By replacing exploitation with renewal our needs and those of the planet can be reconciled.

'Absolutely excellent. If only every literate person in the Western world would read it.' – John Seymour.

'An important book which goes wider and deeper than most green books in considering the causes and solutions of the crises facing mankind.' – Clive Ponting.

The Race for Riches

Jeremy Seabrook

With extraordinary passion and insight, Jeremy Seabrook interweaves the techniques of novel, documentary and polemic to lay bare the myths of modern economics and the empty values which underpin our society. We see the reality of today's world manifested in the lives of ordinary people everywhere, be they in London, Wales, or India. He gives the lie to a myth of progress which offers people an illusion of relief from poverty – a poverty which, instead of being transformed into sufficiency, is deftly turned into another form of privation. The constant factor is the multiple and varied way in which humanity is wasted in this malign project. Everywhere we find the same promise of relief from insecurity and scarcity: yet the reality is always immiseration.

Such development can never emancipate. It can change the nature of poverty, but can never free people from it. Even the richest have a desperate urgency to acquire which has nothing to do with human need, but instead is part of a soulless system which we inhabit and which animates us. We can no longer distinguish between our own hunger for possessions, and that system's insatiable search for profit. There is in fact no problem of poverty – or there would not be, but for the far more intractable problem of wealth and its abusive and monopolistic control of the necessities of the poor.

We must puncture the pretensions of the rich: we must de-mystify wealth, and remove its sacred aura. Our objective: the green project of a satisfying plenty for all. The race for riches by passes the more modest and achievable goal of sufficiency, and leads only to mutations of poverty: to loss, dependency, insecurity. The only cure is a liberation into a sustainable harmony with the Earth that bears us all.

This book is about that race, and that cure.

Living Without Cruelty

Mark Gold

Recipes by Sarah Brown

'Living without Cruelty', 'Beauty Without Cruelty' and the 'Cruelty-Free' consumer campaign are three national campaigns run by the major animal welfare and vegetarian pressure groups and charities. This book encapsulates the arguments of all these campaigns.

The book argues with passion for a commitment to a cruelty-free lifestyle as part of a commitment to a radical green awareness. Mark Gold shows how our everyday living can have cruel and often unforeseen consequences for animals and humans alike. Topics covered include animal suffering, human health, vivisection, entertainment, pets and clothing.

The conclusions are positive and up-beat. The author emphasises the practical alternatives that are available to us in our daily lifestyle – in the kitchen, around the house, the ways we bring up our children, and so on. The book features product listings and a resource guide.

TV cook SARAH BROWN has contributed a collection of original recipes, helping the reader to put theory into delicious practice on the meal table.

'A handy guide to animal welfare and the personal routes a consumer or campaigner can take to the business of living without cruetly' – Richard North, The Independent.

'Real food for thought' – Daily Telegraph.

'This helpful book powerfully explains how our lives are interrelated with animals, how we share a common planet' – Colin Spencer.

'Just what we have all been waiting for' – The Vegetarian.

C for Chemicals
Chemical hazards and how to avoid them

Michael Birkin and Brian Price

A lay guide to all the chemicals most likely to be encountered in everyday life – in kitchen, bathroom, living room and bedroom, in DIY and building work, in the garage, the garden and the greenhouse. There are A–Z listings for quick and easy reference. Substances are listed alphabetically either by chemical name, or by substance or application (eg oven cleaners, hair care, etc).

The authors answer the consumer's worries and questions on countless topics: toys, cleaners, cosmetics, fabrics, bleaches, paints, wood treatments, weedkillers, insecticides, fertilisers, insulation materials, petrol, etc, etc. They give up-to-date information gathered specially for this book from a wide range of international sources, much of it not easily available to the general public.

The emphasis throughout is on safe alternatives to dangerous substances and practices. As much a practical guide to the alternatives as a handbook of dangers, the book includes a gardener's guide to safe disease and pest control.

Where appropriate, advice is given on how to pressurise manufacturers and what to ask for.

MIKE BIRKIN and BRIAN PRICE are environmental consultants and researchers based in the Bristol area.

Spirit for Change

Voices of Hope for a World in Crisis

Christopher Titmuss

Spirituality is often seen as something quite apart from the affairs of this world. Yet many people who are engaged in the struggle for social change also have a powerful spiritual commitment.

In this challenging and enlightening book, Christopher Titmuss talks to a number of people, many of them already well-known for their political and social activity, about the profound spiritual motivation which inspires them.

They also talk of the crisis which is threatening the planet, and the kinds of constructive response they have been able to make at a time when hope is often in short supply.

Christopher Titmuss, a former Buddhist monk, teaches insight meditation retreats worldwide and is a counsellor on spiritual, psychological and global issues. He is an active supporter of the international Green movement.

The conversations in this book are with Satish Kumar, Joanna Macy, U Nu, Fleana Bergonzi, Jonathon Porritt, Jean Pink, John Seed, Jim Perkins, Sulak Sivaraksa, Mary Lightfoot, A. T. Ariyaratna, Fritjof Capra, Christina Feldman, and Roger Walsh.